CW01663903

To Dorothy,

with best wishes,

Jane Evans

(JANE EVANS)

(MARTIN EVANS)

Reflections

For Daniel and Jessica

With many thanks to our friend Neil Roberts, Professor Emeritus of English Literature at Sheffield University, for his very helpful comments on first drafts of the poems.

First published in Great Britain 2023

Text copyright © Martin Evans
Illustrations © Jane Evans

The moral rights of the illustrator and author have been asserted.

No part of this book may be used or reproduced in any manner whatsoever without written permission from the publisher except in the case of brief quotations embodied in critical articles or reviews.

Ekphrastic Endeavours, Cambridge, UK

Stamford Press
3–4 Wellington Lane
Stamford PE9 1QB

ISBN 978-0-9553-6792-2

Printed in the UK by Biddles

Reflections

Chinese brush paintings by Jane Evans | Poems on the painting by Martin Evans

Introduction

The Paintings

It was somewhat daunting to be asked to name my forty-five favourite paintings, out of the many I have created during my artistic career, for Martin to write about. Some of my paintings did readily suggest themselves: these include the cat, which I have used as my logo for several years; and some whose subject matter is close to my heart, such as the painting of New Hall (now Murray Edwards College) where I was a student and other Cambridge scenes, including St John's, where Martin studied. I would also include in this category Glastonbury Tor, which reminds me of visits to my sister. This book also contains several pictures of the Haute-Loire; I was spoilt for choice here as I have painted it so frequently! Lastly, I included a few that could be seen as signature pieces: the two birds side by side, the snail and the frog.

All the paintings are Chinese inks and colours on *xuan*. Pastel has also been used in 'The Cam in Winter' and gold leaf has been used in 'Near Pokhara'. The red seal or chop, depicting my name in Chinese seal script, was designed for me by my teacher, Professor Chen Bing Sun.

Jane Evans

The Poems

Jane has sold very many paintings over the years to very satisfied customers and we also have more at home, awaiting her next exhibition. While we have generally adhered to the principle that her best works should always be offered for sale, she has generously agreed that some of her paintings to which I am particularly attached may hang permanently on our own walls. I know which of Jane's paintings I like best, but what would be her choice? Which of her works have given her the most satisfaction, on completion or during execution? While our selections did not always coincide, which I found intriguing, I nevertheless set myself the task of writing a poem for each painting that Jane had chosen. I must leave it to the reader to decide how far my arrangements of words do justice to Jane's arrangements of brushstrokes and colours.

Martin Evans

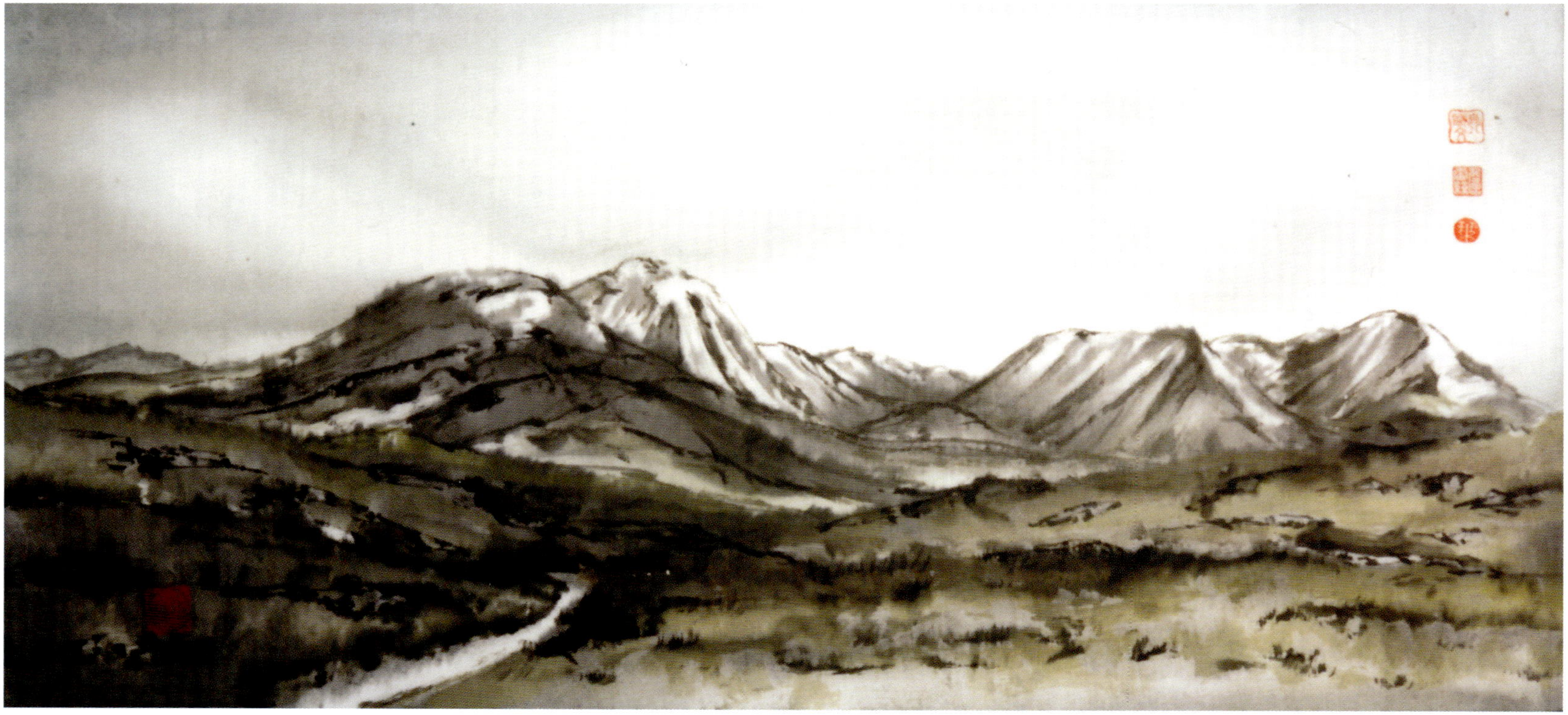

Rannoch Moor

The lines are rock-scratched, the colours leached sparse,
the wash doesn't dry on Rannoch's grey grass.
Cold bones of dead hills show white from afar,
a stream cuts the foreground in an old scar.

Here winds come howling in packs of wild dogs,
raising ghouls and demons up from the bogs.
This is the earth's end, there's nought to live for
on this "God-forgotten, man-forsworn, wild" moor.

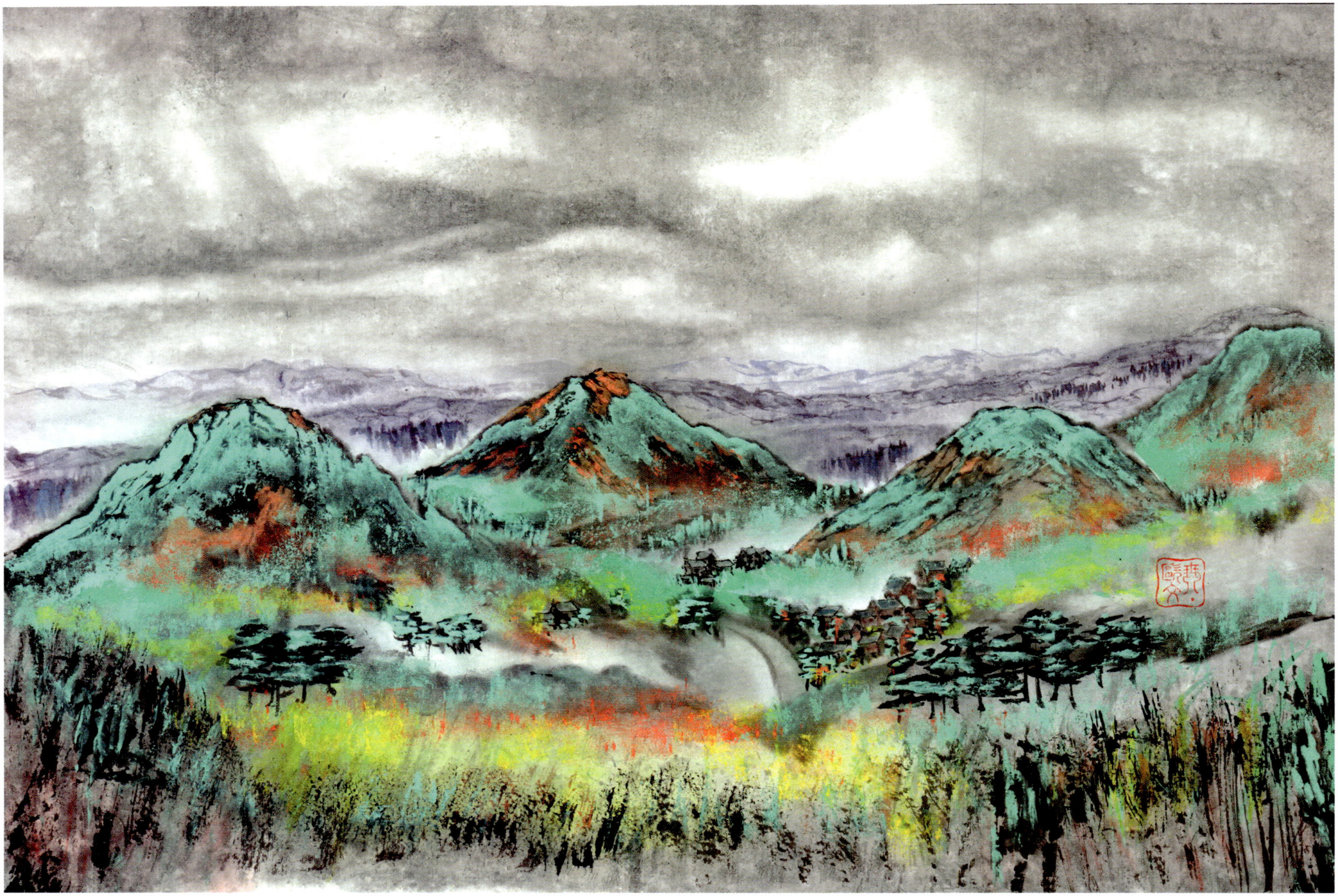

View from Raffy

Driving up Meygal on a gloomy day,
shrunk in on oneself by the pressing pines,
comes the revelation – from Raffy's modest
standpoint – that the entire world has been unrolled
at your feet: flung far out to horizon
after horizon.

The vastness of an ocean's depth awaits
your plunging in to cross time and space
and swim amid the bubbled *sucs* of Vulcan's
works inside the Earth, still hot and lava-licked
…or is it just autumn's fiery splashes now
burning on the trees?

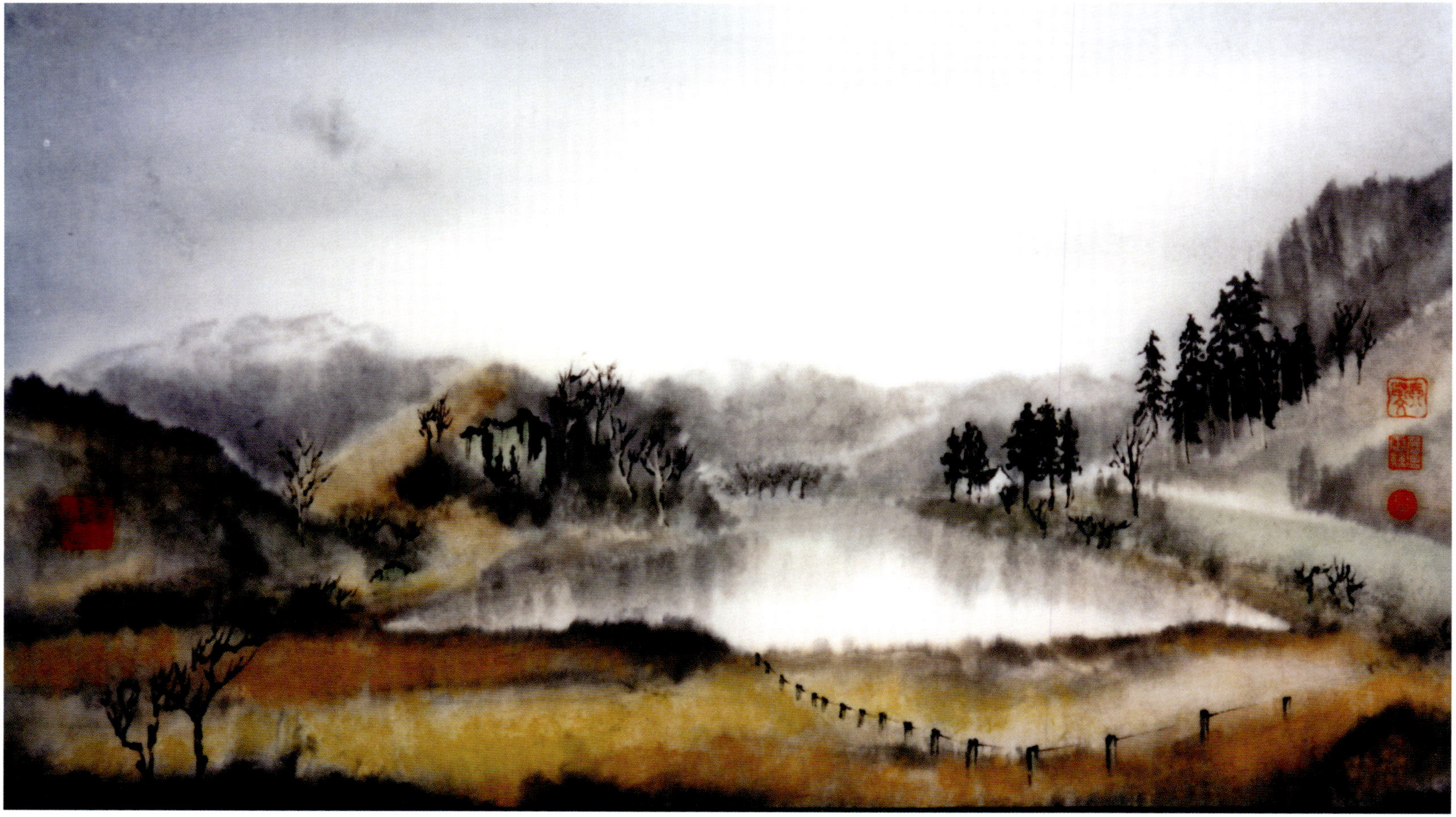

Loch Duich

Soft fingertip of the western sea
held gently in the palm of the land
by mountains with caps of fading white.

A quiet cottage contemplating
spring stirrings in a placid pool that
mirrors in mist hints of brighter light.

Birches' hands, winter-rigid, waiting,
tall pines gathering, always ready,
heather browns, the tints of Scotland's skin.

In this corner of Loch Duich can
be found the *chi* of Highland mornings.

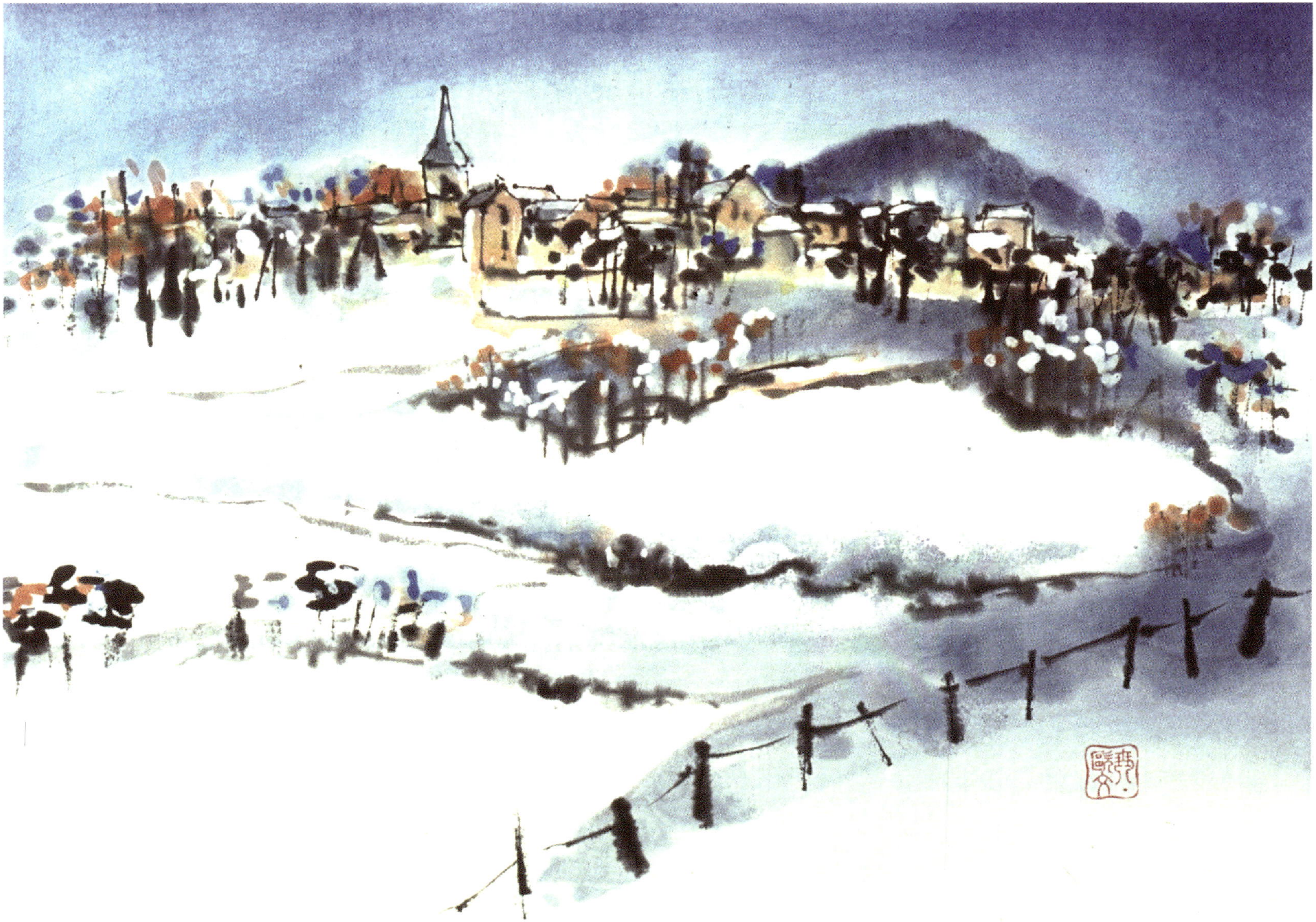

Boussoulet

Old stone houses pick out the ridgeline
softened by a sprinkle of wintry trees,
the slopes below sparkle with snow
that seems so luxuriously deep.
There's a nice church steeple,
the sky's a deep bright blue –
a photo postcard view –
and it was true
that day from
this spot.

But

every year
there are fewer here:
not a hundred souls now left
high among the rocks from which
the young have fled, out from under the
heavy shroud of cold cloud that will obscure
the village for so long so often, and having to endure
all the world passing through without stopping (even *Le Tour*
came here once). Not many, it seems, want a postcard of Boussoulet.

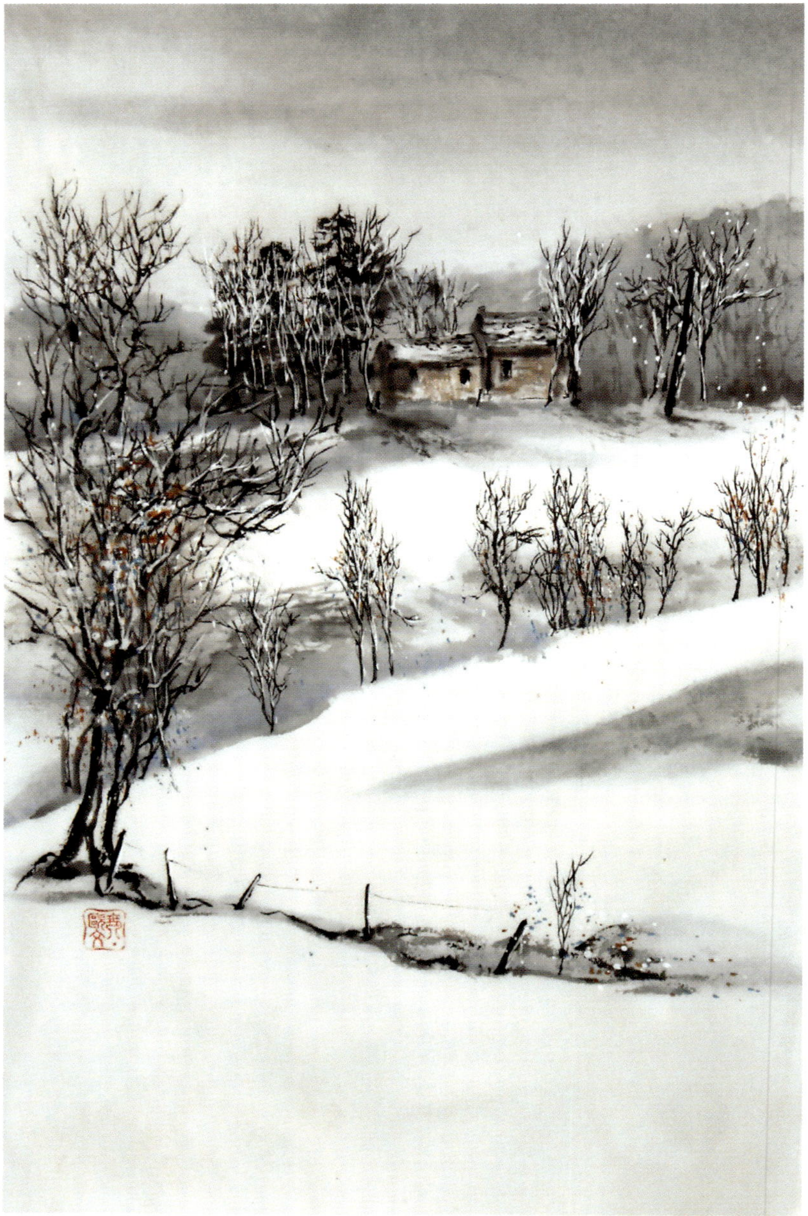

Our Neighbours' House

We'd walk down the lane as evening fell
and find the sun was waiting there
to wrap us in its welcoming glow
in the home of Colette and Gilbert.
Same seats always, by the window;
white wine for Jane, whisky for me
and whisky was his tipple too,
with new labels for me to see.
Now and then Colette would leave us
to bring fresh snacks on a new platter;
Gilbert would top up all our glasses
and we'd recap on our natter.
They liked to hear our English view
on this and that, all kinds of things;
he was fast, I hadn't the words
for all the 'cabbages and kings',
no problem for Jane, but for me
Colette spoke slowly with great care.
We supped on fine philosophies,
drank with humour and with rare
wisdom till, brimming with the evening's warmth,
we'd stand up, say we had to go;
usual jokes about getting lost
or our way blocked by summer snow.
Sometimes this meant another sip
'to keep us going till we got back',
even though our house was only
a few hundred yards up the track.

Now the shutters are closed, doors locked,
the house huddled in winter sleep.
We talk, as we walk by below,
of all the thoughts that we must keep
of our good friends, now long gone:
he is no more and she's in care.
As we trudge back over the snow
the sky is darker everywhere.

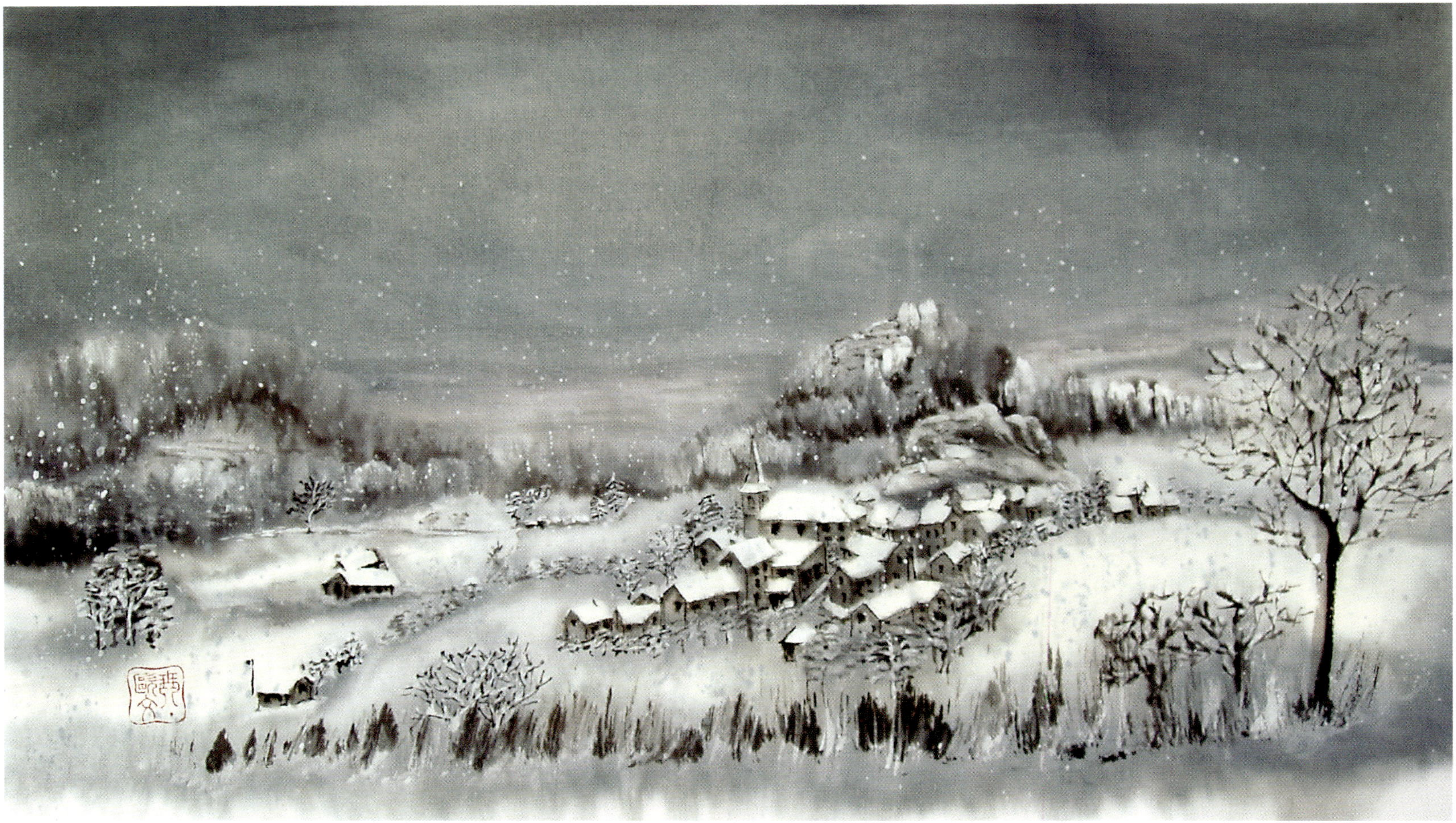

Queyrières in the Snow

This hilltop hamlet huddles round a stump,
its houses clustered in a mushroom clump.
You'll find near the church in the tiny square
a panel that tells of the hardening lump
that stuck in the throat puking liquid stone;
from this choking earth was born Queyrières.

Seen from far off in a snow-brightened light
against dark skies, it's a Christmas card sight
but don't try to make a seasonal trip
to this soft nest, feather-snuggled in white;
up there the wind cuts, it's glacier cold,
Queyrières barely breathes in winter's grip.

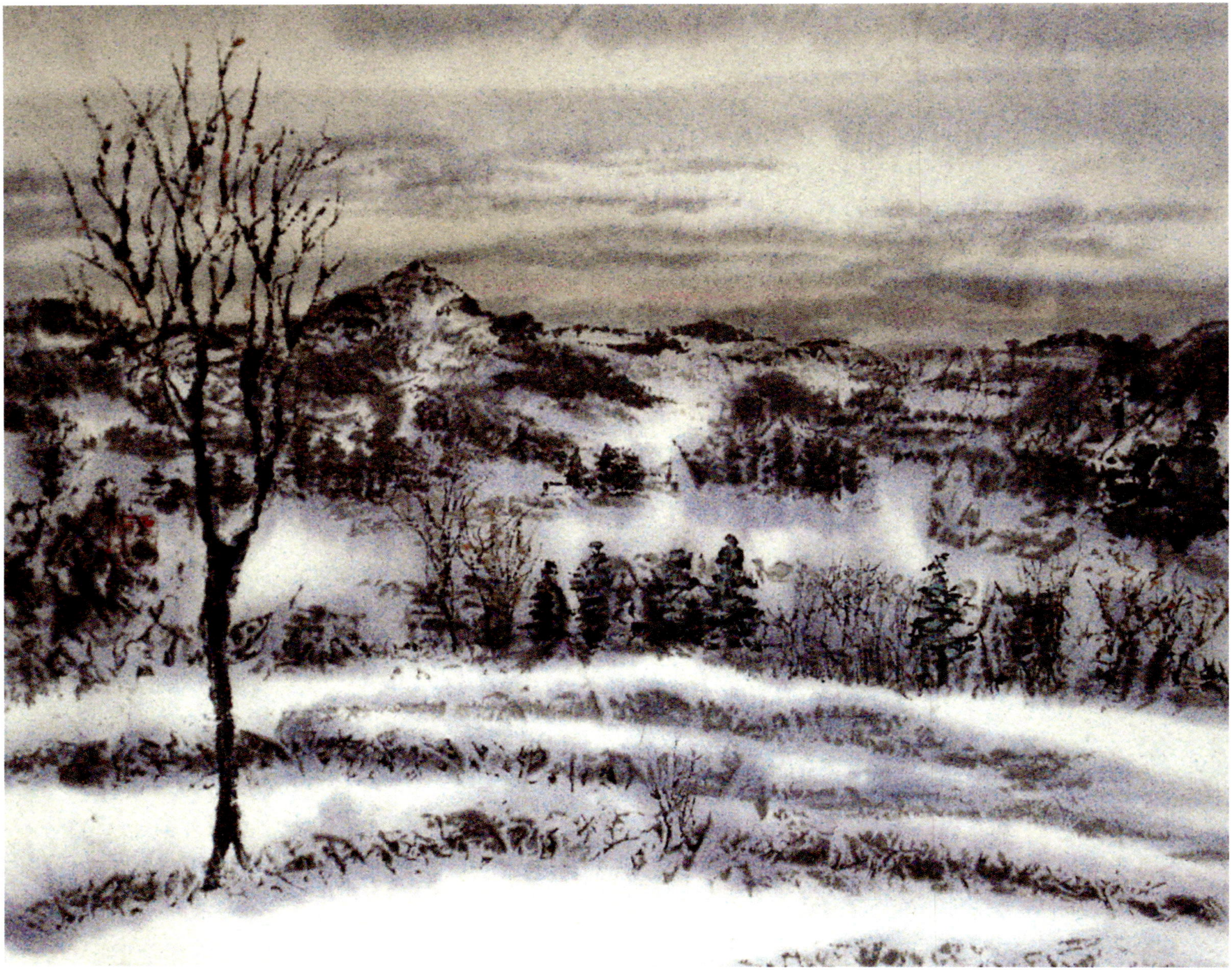

Winter in the Valley of the Auze

This scene could be
from centuries ago,
all traces of time
buried by snow.

It's the same ghostly mould
on the land's wrinkled face,
but did it bring despair
that scarce hoarded fare
might not be enough
to keep man and beast
until the spring?
It's the same white fur
on hills dark with trees,
but did it bring fear
of packs coming near
and rib thin wolves
taking new-born kids
or a straying child?

Now, our futures are starved
by the gnawing dread
that in the winters to come,
there may be no snow at all.

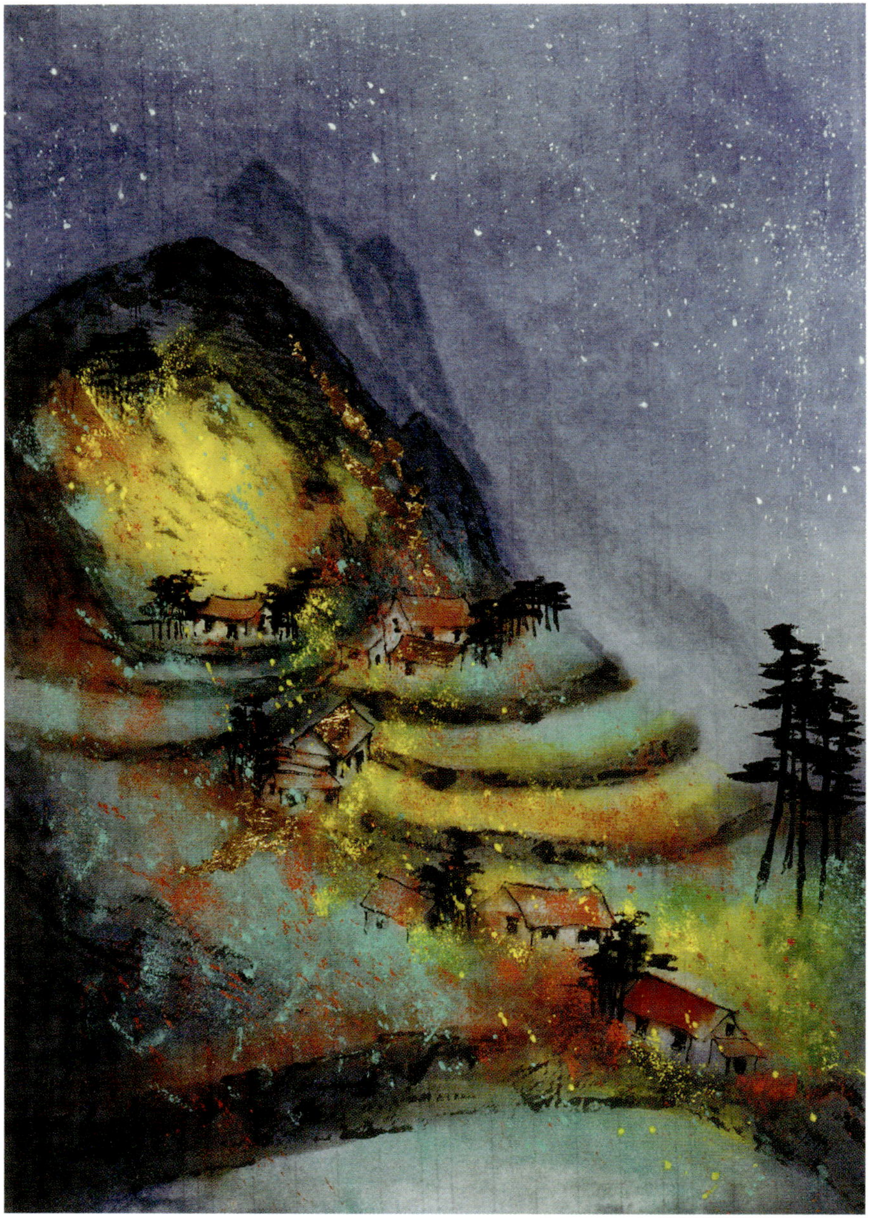

Near Pokhara

Returning home one evening, quite alone,
from meagre fields after a day of toil,
stepping along the terrace walls of stone
that stopped the rain from taking all the soil,
in the gloom she slipped,
felt her ankle bones crack, let out a cry,
then slumped down to free her foot, if she could,
and hoping that someone might soon come by
she looked to the hill where her village stood.

She gasped, for she could see that from within
the hill, the golden glow told in prayer
was shining through the earth's translucent skin:
by these ramparts of the Himalaya
a Buddha was buried
right under their feet and she'd been chosen,
the only one to be shown its lustre
for the light was gone, the hill dark, frozen,
and willing all the strength she could muster,
she stood up slowly, felt no pain at all;
she couldn't go home, they'd not understand,
so turned and started for that mountain wall:
she had to find the wisest in the land
– by the stars, up there.

High in the land of eternal snow, she
was found, near dead, close by the *gompa* gate;
gently, monks led her to the Lama; he
of deepest learning could foresee her fate
and saw in her there burned a golden flame:
this most holy woman of pure clear light,
who had no abode nor even a name,
would now live here as her lifelong right.
She could not speak, no
words would come, not then nor evermore;
all the rest of her days she'd paint that scene
in the most sublime of *thangkas*, sure
this way the world would know what she had seen.

Duck

Not a duck
birders with binoculars could name:
American Black, but the beak?
Common Scoter, but with those feet?
It's The Duck
learned lexicographers use
to define, for all birds called ducks,
their duckness.

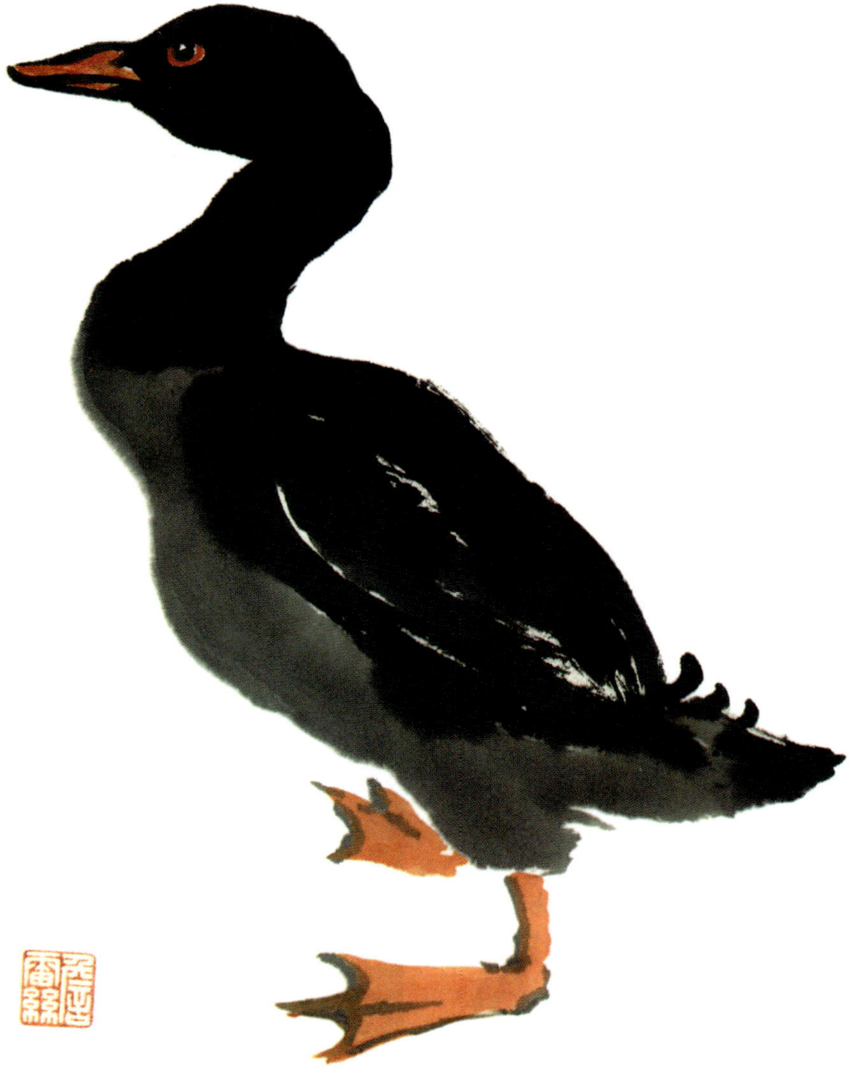

Milk Bottle with Snail

This portrait
of our mountaineering
mollusc
in the greys and black
of rocks in snow,
shows it high
on the South Col
eyeing up
the overhang
of the Hillary Step;
a few more squeezes
of its flexi-foot
and it will summit.
The bottle's empty,
the view mundane,
but as Mallory said,
it's because it's there.

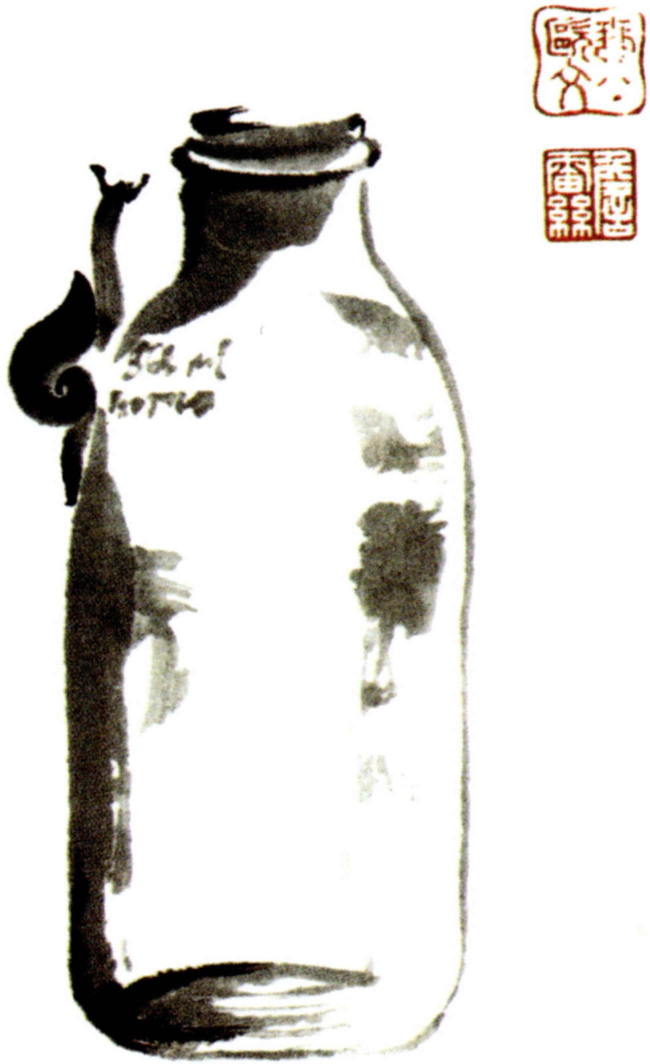

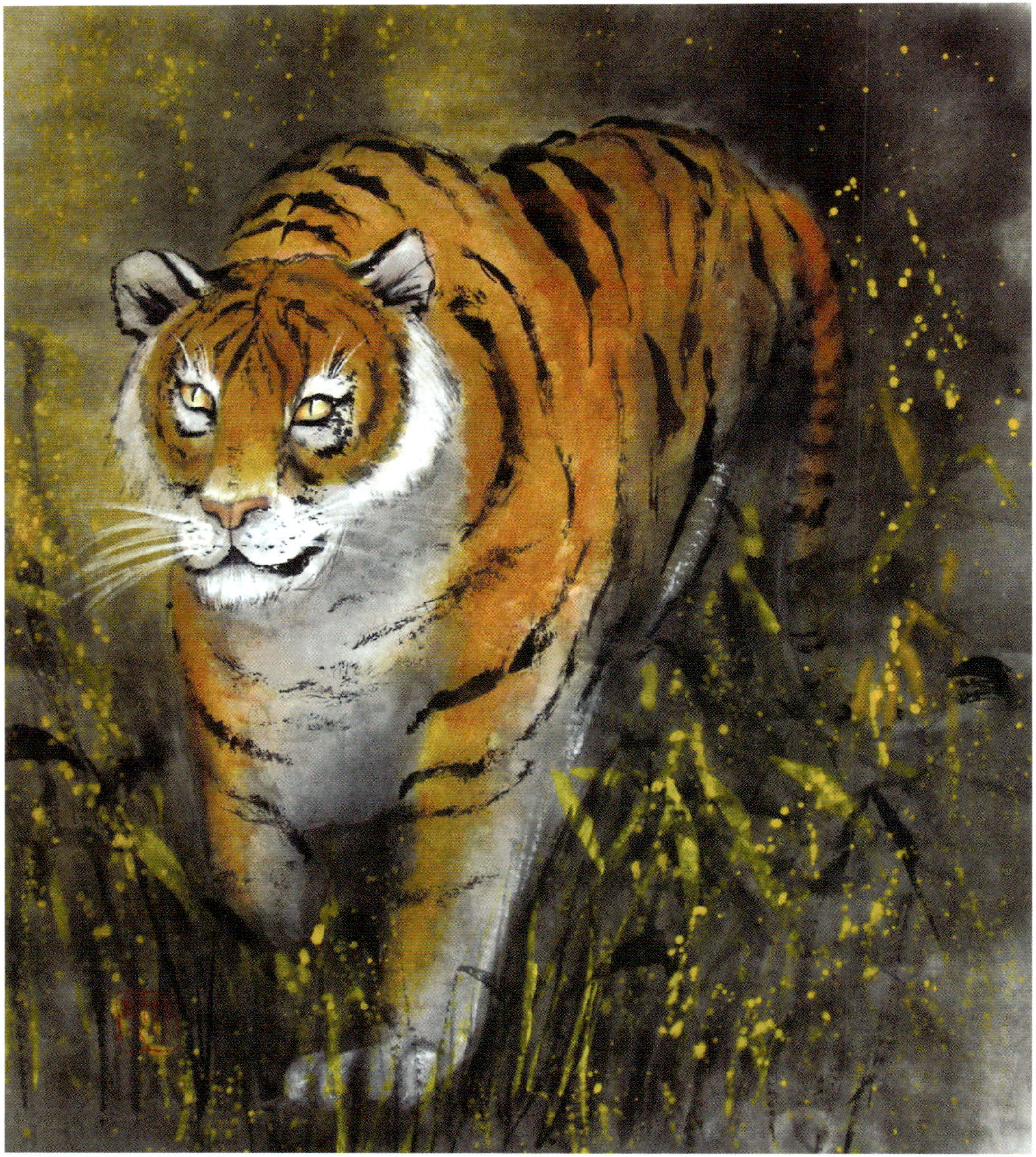

Tiger

I am blocked by fear and cannot go near
this burning beast of the night.

Long ago caught for the printed page by
a better poet than me;
it’s a pointless move to try to improve
on his “fearful symmetry”.

So I’ll back away, but before I go
I’d like to suggest to you
the opposite page does justice to Blake
for there stalks a tyger true.

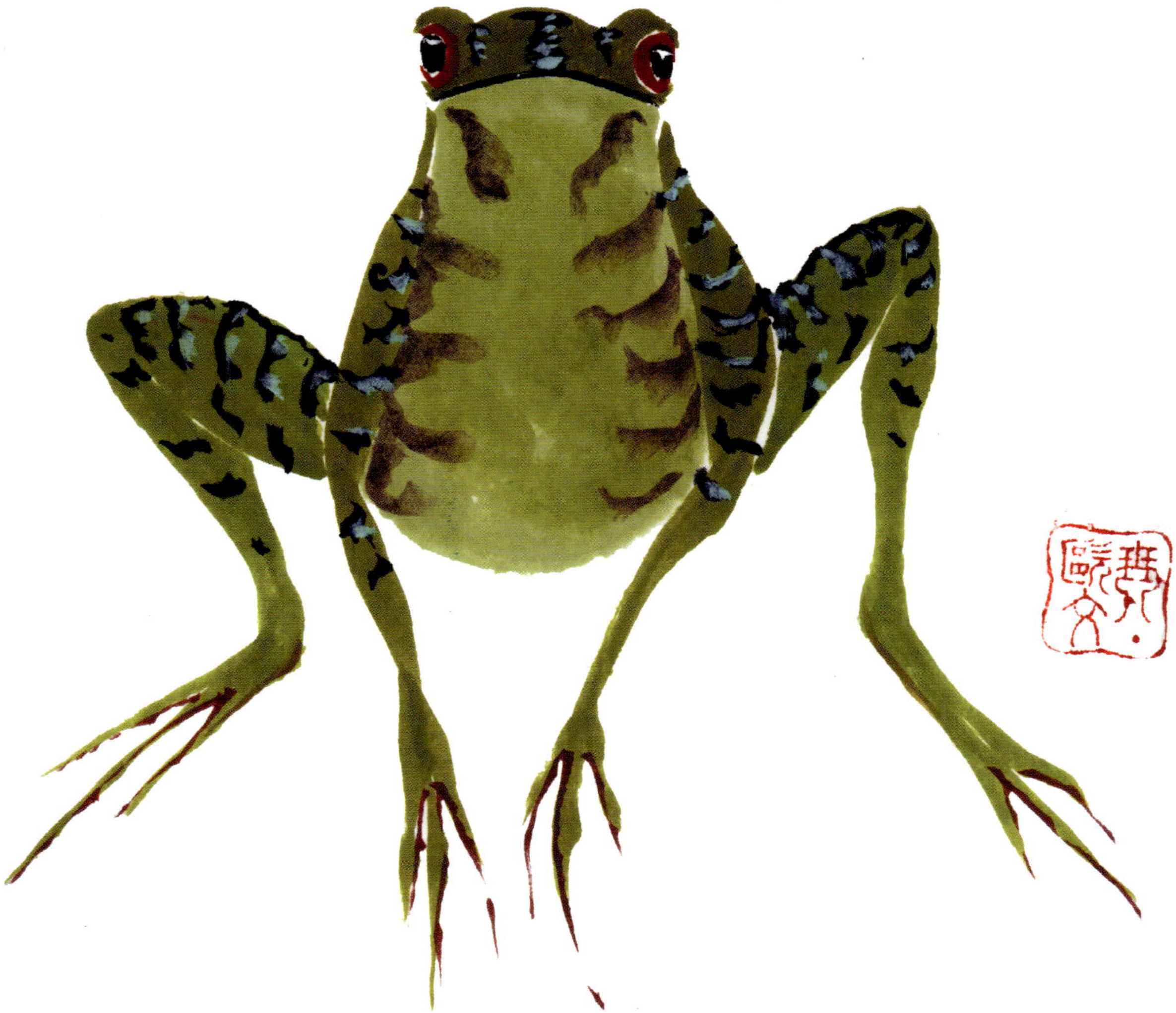

Frog

I'm sorry to tell you this
(I don't know if you've heard)
but like the rest of your kind
you look a bit absurd.

It's all those bits bulging out
on rather spindly legs,
your staring sideways eyes,
your bellies fat as kegs.

Figure of fun you may be
but we love the way you look,
it's why we keep you hopping
through all our children's books.

We're always pleased to see you
unlike your cousin the toad
so we're really sorry to find you
flattened on the road.

You are, you know, too squashable –
not a good thing to be –
so don't just sit there blinking,
please jump away and stay free.

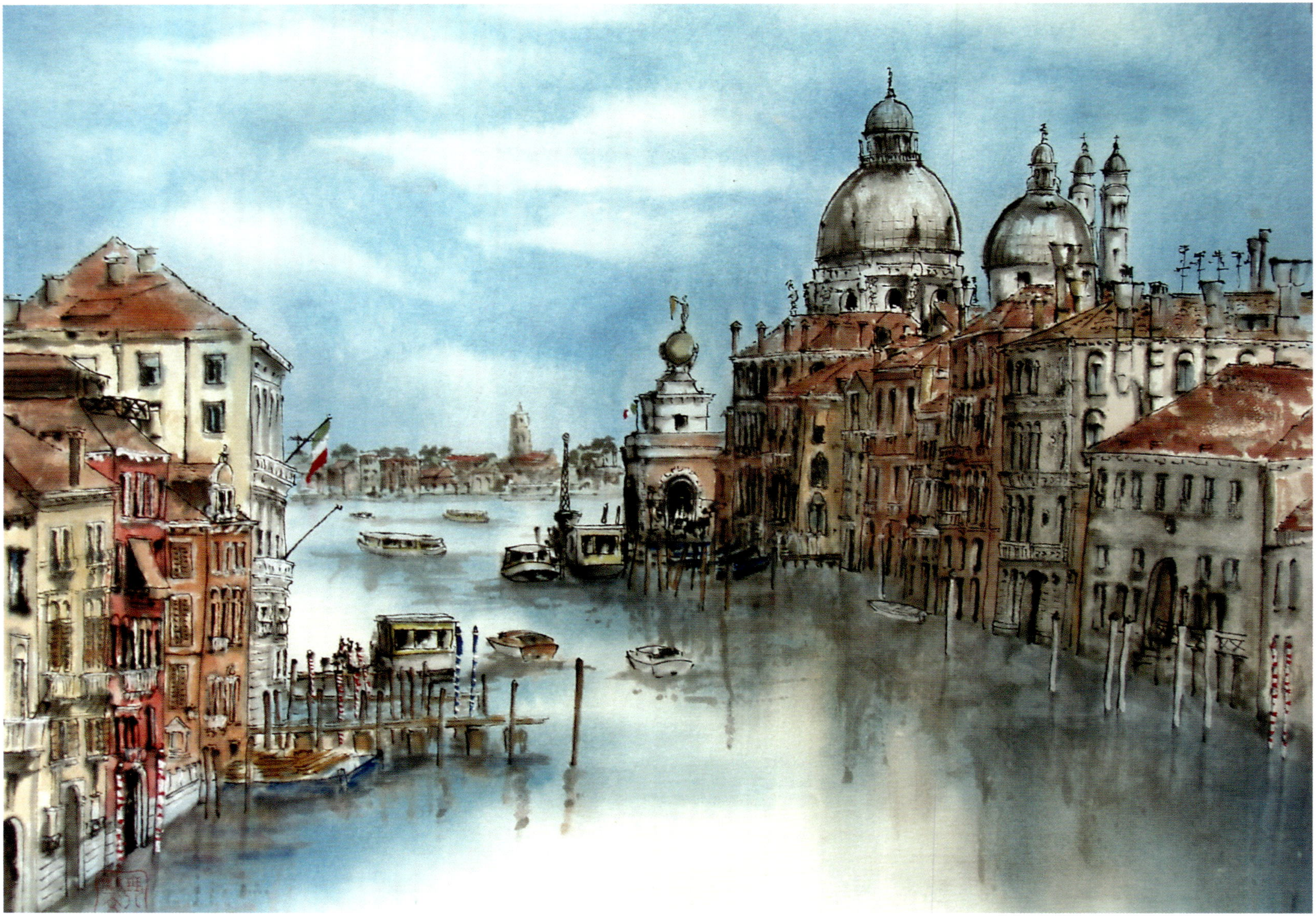

The Grand Canal

Unreal city on unearthly island
its magnificence floats into the sky
and sinks ever deeper into its mud;
this crazy construction of wet and dry.

Over-gilded, -sculpted, -towered and -domed
unbelievable palaces of ghosts
whose flaunted wealth and basilica pride
sit carelessly on mangrove shores of posts.

This mermaid of fantastical beauty
swimming blue sunshine between sky and sea
flashing impossibly glorious art,
can she really live for eternity?

Shark frenzies of selfie-taking tourists
hunting for all the treasures they can find,
while rusting balconies, peeling facades
look down on darkening waters behind.

Let it go, this renaissance mandala
it's destined to be washed away by time;
so will it be forever remembered –
a fabled city at its most sublime.

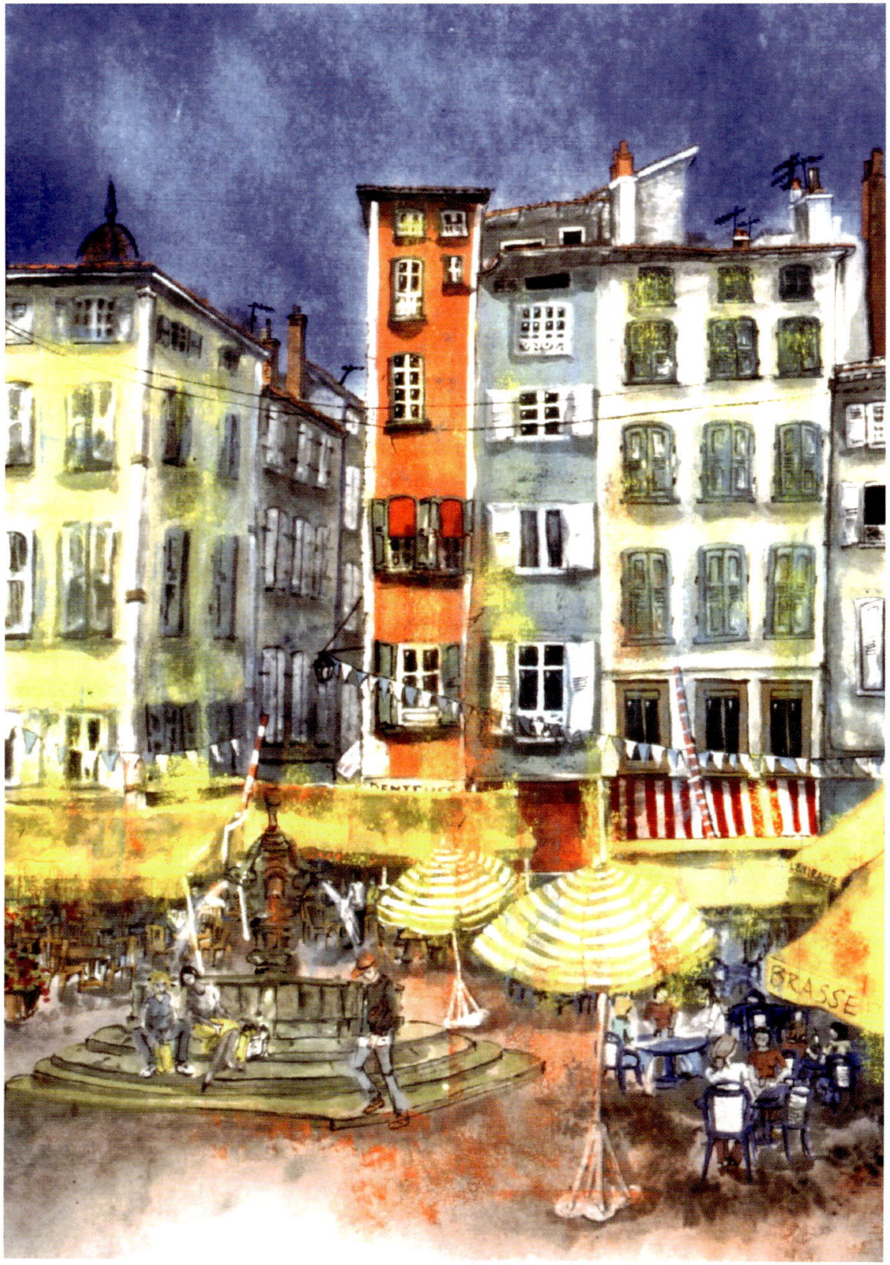
BRASSE

Café Afternoon

If you want to watch the world go by,
the Place du Plot's the place to go:
under café shades when the sun's up high,
you can feel its magic as time goes slow.
Cracked shutters hung on bright-paint walls
look down on the oldest mart in France,
clatter and chatter from centuries call;
this place isn't special just by chance.

Hurrying past or strolling through,
they are the innocent and streetwise,
Ponots, tourists, some like us two –
quasi-locals in disguise.
The old, the young, the weak, the strong,
they all come here to walk or wait,
including those whose life's gone wrong
because of cards dealt out by fate.

For those whose minds are troubled
or must live their lives in wheelchairs,
or stumble by all huddled,
they'll find Le Puy is always theirs;
for it doesn't matter who you are,
what you've done or where you've been,
this quirky town will set no bar
and will surely take you in.

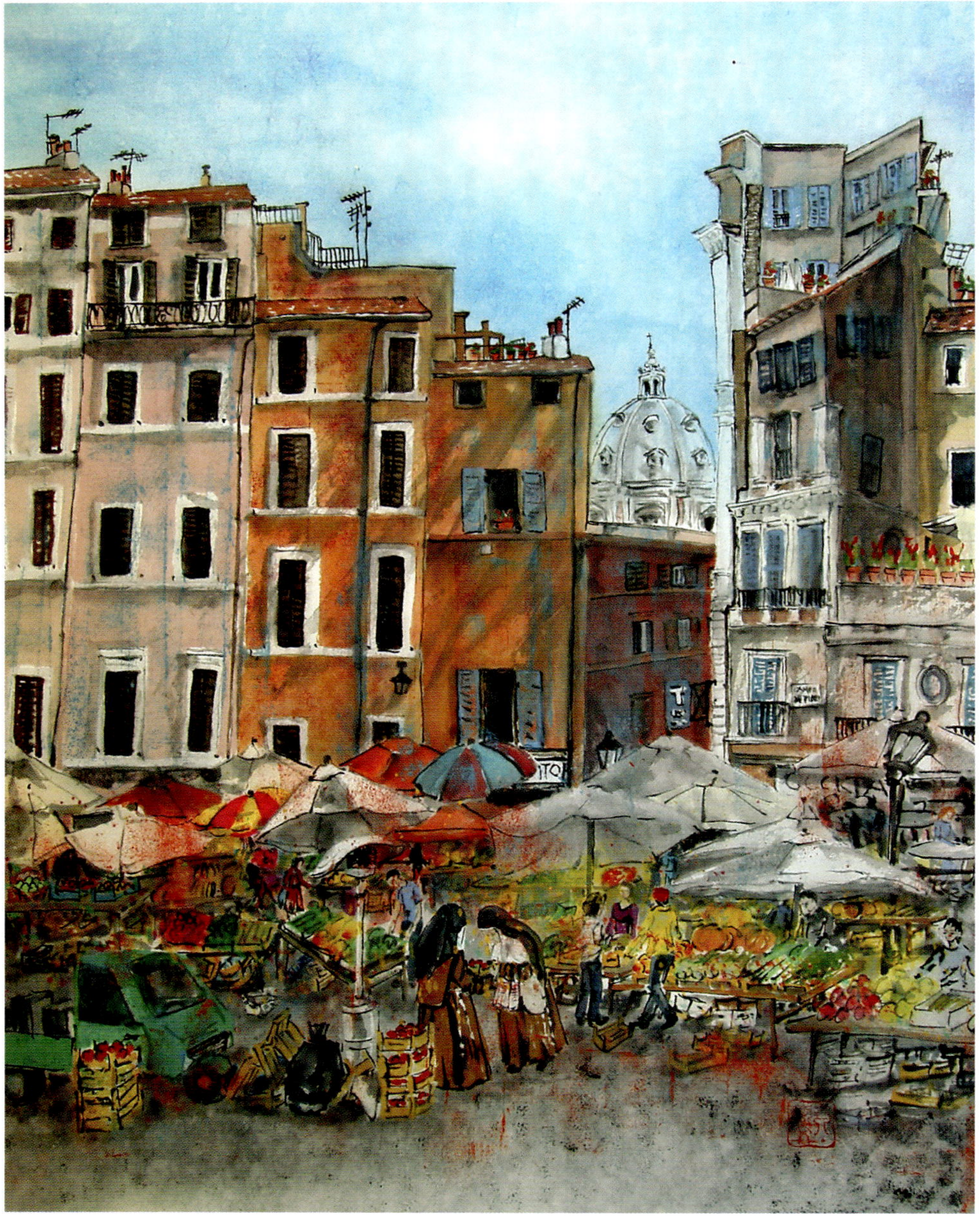

Campo de Fiori

Those days: the metro clatters, her voice calls
“Garbatella, Pyramide, Circo
Massimo, Colosseo …”
walking, walking, warm roofs, rust red walls.

Cobbles, cafés, shaded tables – there’s one
free, let’s sit down, looks like a good spot
almost where we were last time;
same places always – our Rome in the sun.

Paint box open, water in pot, fresh pad,
everyday coffee, rare summer cigar,
pencil lines inking, colour washing;
it’s coming on nicely, not much to add.

Waiter en route stops to look, nods his head,
new customer there can wait for a bit;
this one’s good – she’s got Fiori just right –
maybe the best he’s seen, it will be said.

Montaged fruits, flowers and veg
awnings, stalls, boxes, trays
stuff below out the way
crushed stems, curled leaves at feet,
people prodding and poking,
sometimes picking and paying,
bustling with bags and baskets,
moving on to next display:
bees between expectant blooms.

What are these good Sisters up to
beneath St Andrew’s stony gaze,
watched by dark-eyed towers of jostling flats
their rooftops abuzz with listening ears?
The traders put something by,
stuff a little old perhaps
or maybe over mottled
but also a bit of fresh:
help them in their charity.
They always come twice a week,
stall to stall like nosing dogs,
a good cause he supposes,
shrugging while his watchful mate
attends to those with money.
The saintly ladies check their haul
wondering if it’s good enough
or this market’s getting meaner.

It’s now tasting a little old,
another half-hour? better not:
Fiori’s done but drying still
and coffee number three’s gone cold.
Time to close the lid, empty pot
catch waiter’s eye and pay the bill.

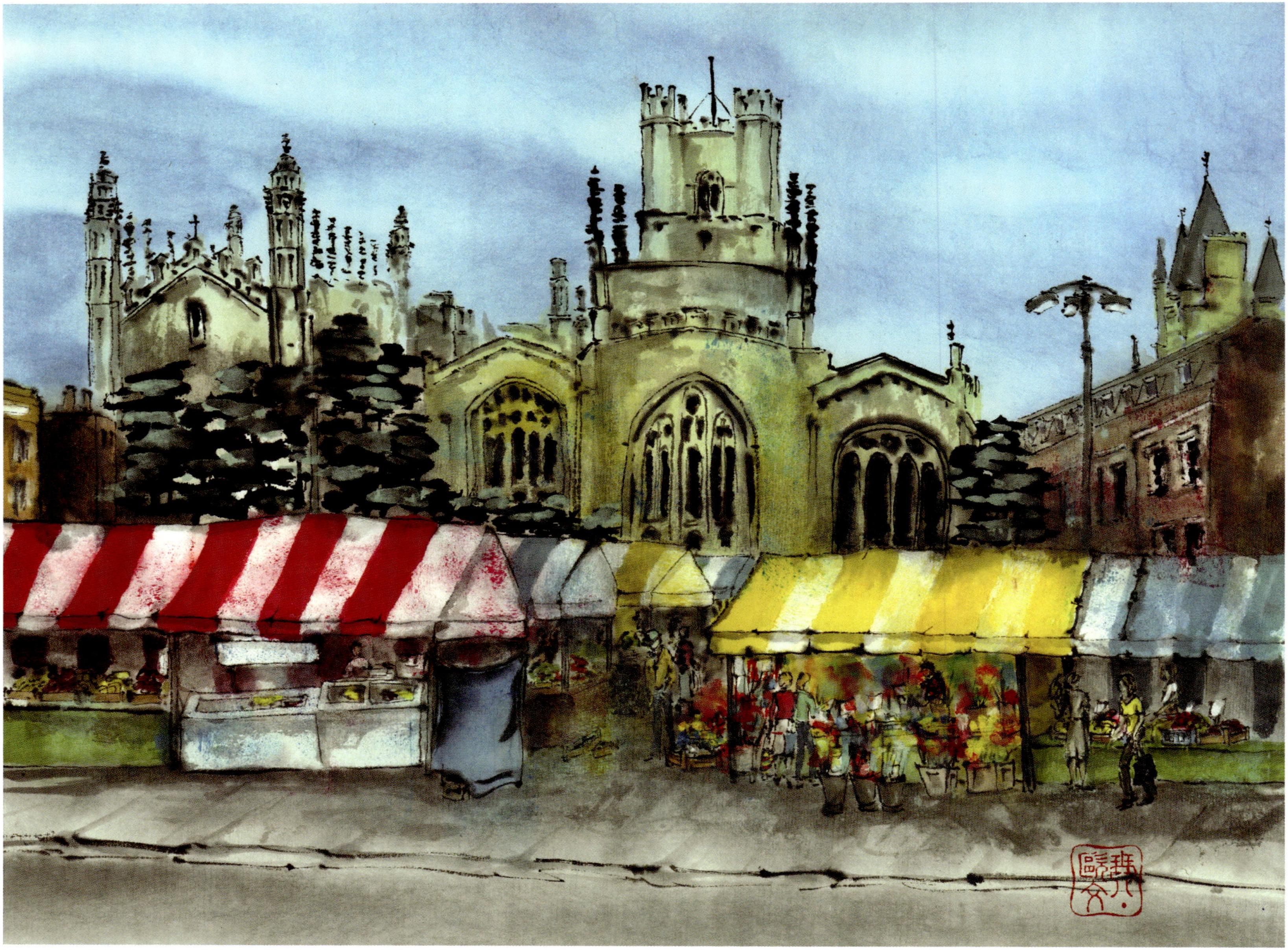

Cambridge Market

Beneath brooding Great St Mary's
Cambridge market spreads its wings,
home each day to a sharp-eyed flock
poking about for all kinds of things:
flowers and fishes, fruit and veg,
cheeses, breads, hats of all types,
assertive T-shirts, loud CDs,
spread out under the awning stripes.

King's and Caius' stand well back from
common commotion in Market Square
that once saw floggings, folk in stocks,
lives choked off in the gallows' snare.
It's the city's lodestone, with miles marked
from Great St Mary's on the London road;
and to earn a degree the dons decree
within three miles for the nights' abode.

The colleges here feed the mind,
the churches look after the soul;
it's the market that for centuries
has kept the Cambridge body whole.

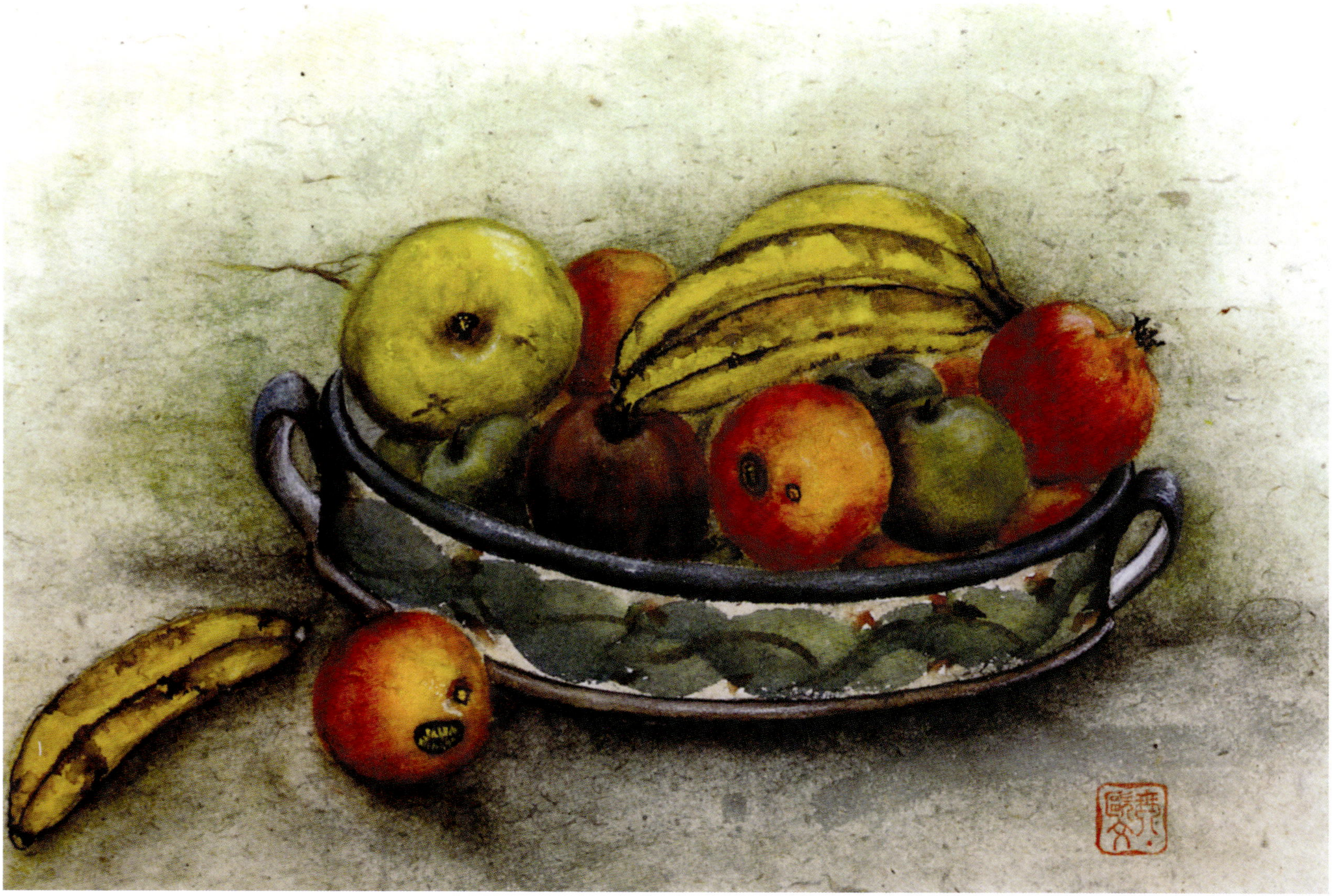

Bowl of Fruit

Bowls of fruit, like jugs of flowers
are classic tests of artists' powers:
can they work the stillness of the scene
to show some glorious life that's been?

The bowl is overfilled
so some of it is spilled:
will that apple roll
or stop bruised beneath the bowl?
If we lift the plate
can we feel its weight?

Has something else been caught,
more than we first thought?
For art is the surprise
of seeing with new eyes.

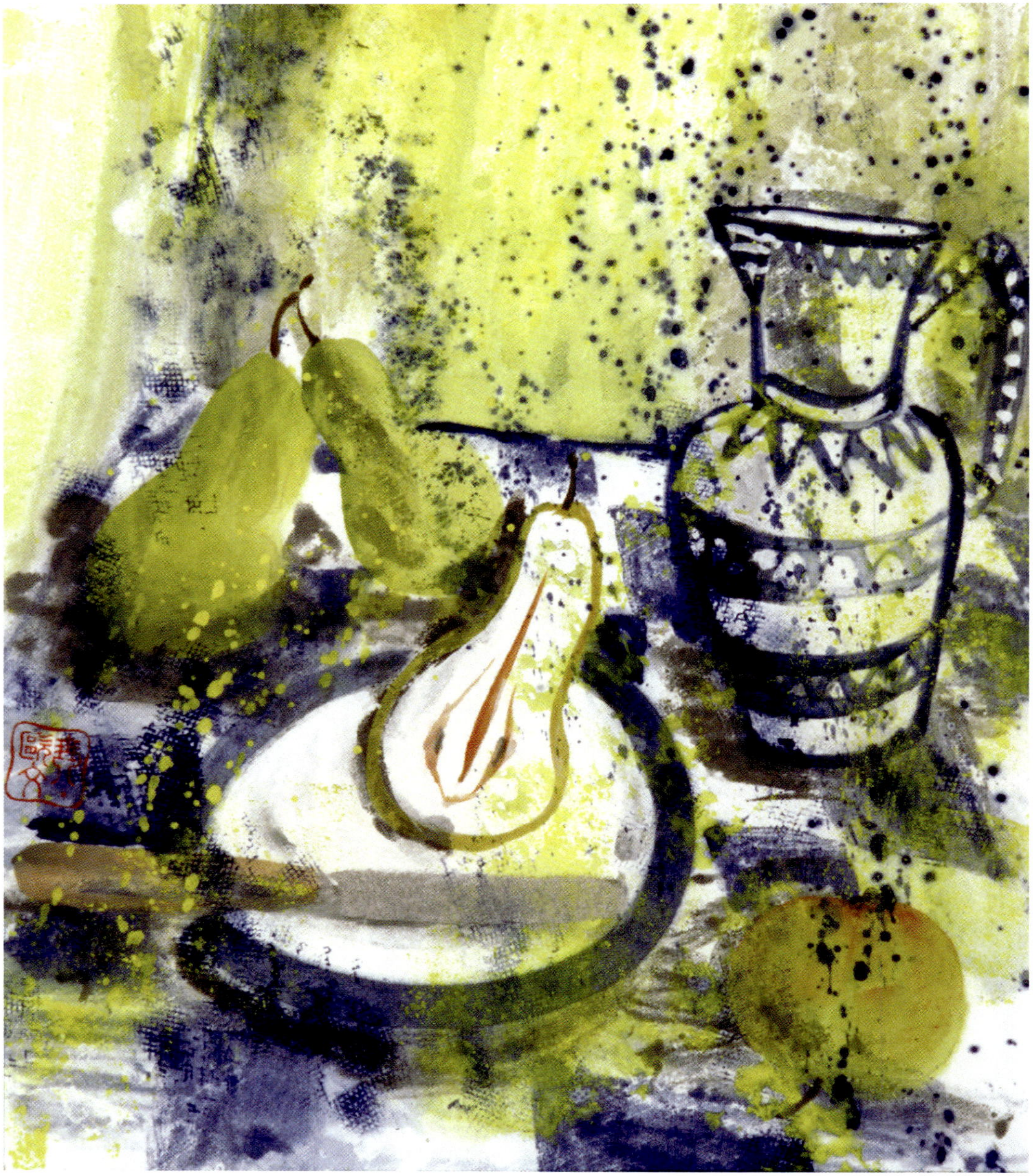

Pear

Freshly cleaved,
how long has half the pear
been open to the air?
Who had the other half
dribbling sweetly on their chin?
And was the hard rough skin
first pared off
(is that knife sharp enough
and where are the peel pieces?)
Or was it gnawed in a sticky jowled
gorging, melon-style
off stage?
And all the while
stands ready that Picasso jug –
full to drink or waiting dustily
for a colour spay of flowers?
The tablecloth, jug and plate
blue and white
look very right
up against the lemon wall:
vinegar and syrup
keep each other in check.
With such art,
can any pear taste as good?

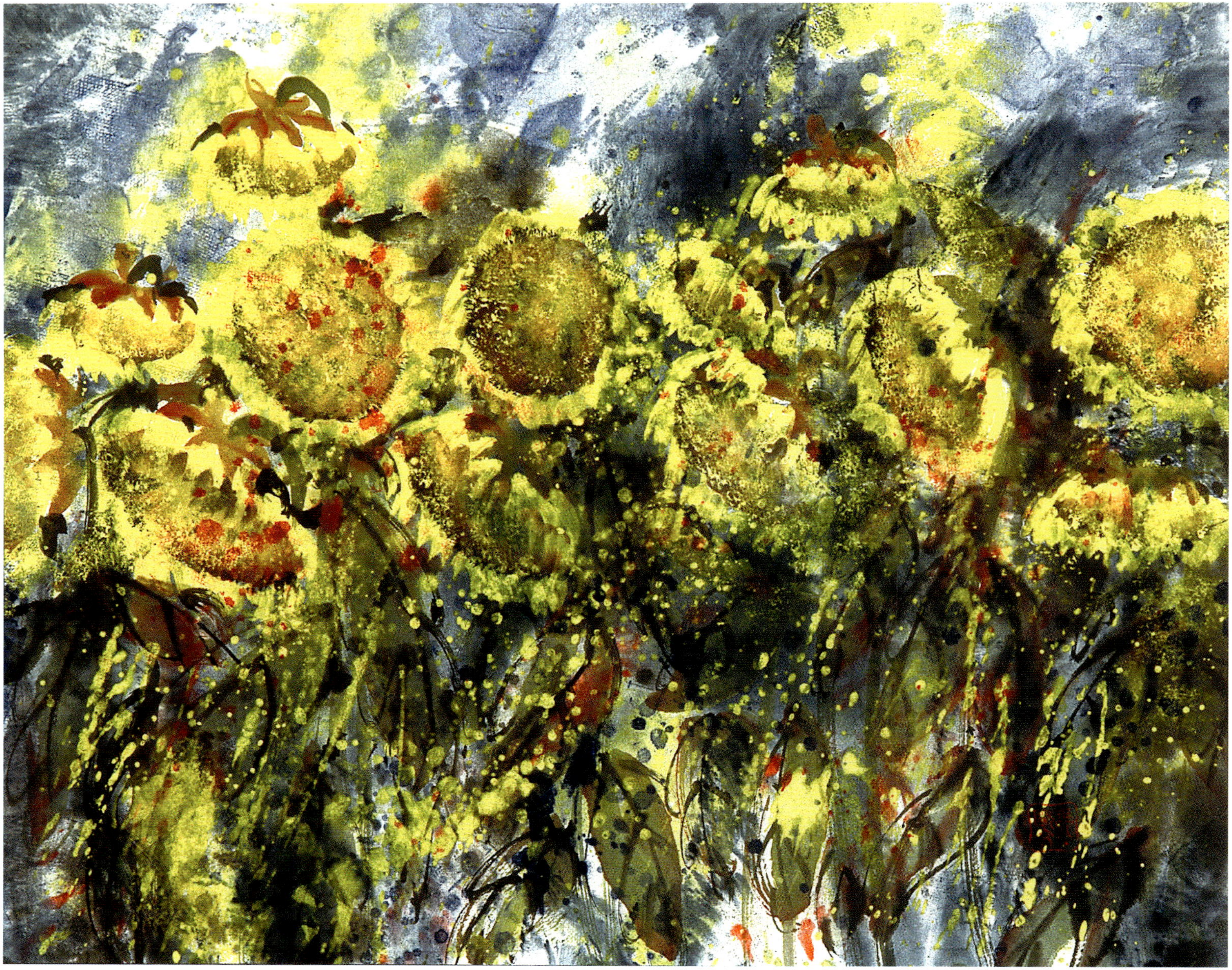

Sunflowers

Whole fields of sunflowers
can be unsettling:
ranks of advancing robots
all turning their unearthly
suns or outsize
insect eyes
in your direction.

This much nearer view
reassures:
a little group of open faces
and bobbing bonnets
bent earnestly inwards
in debate, not interested
in you at all.

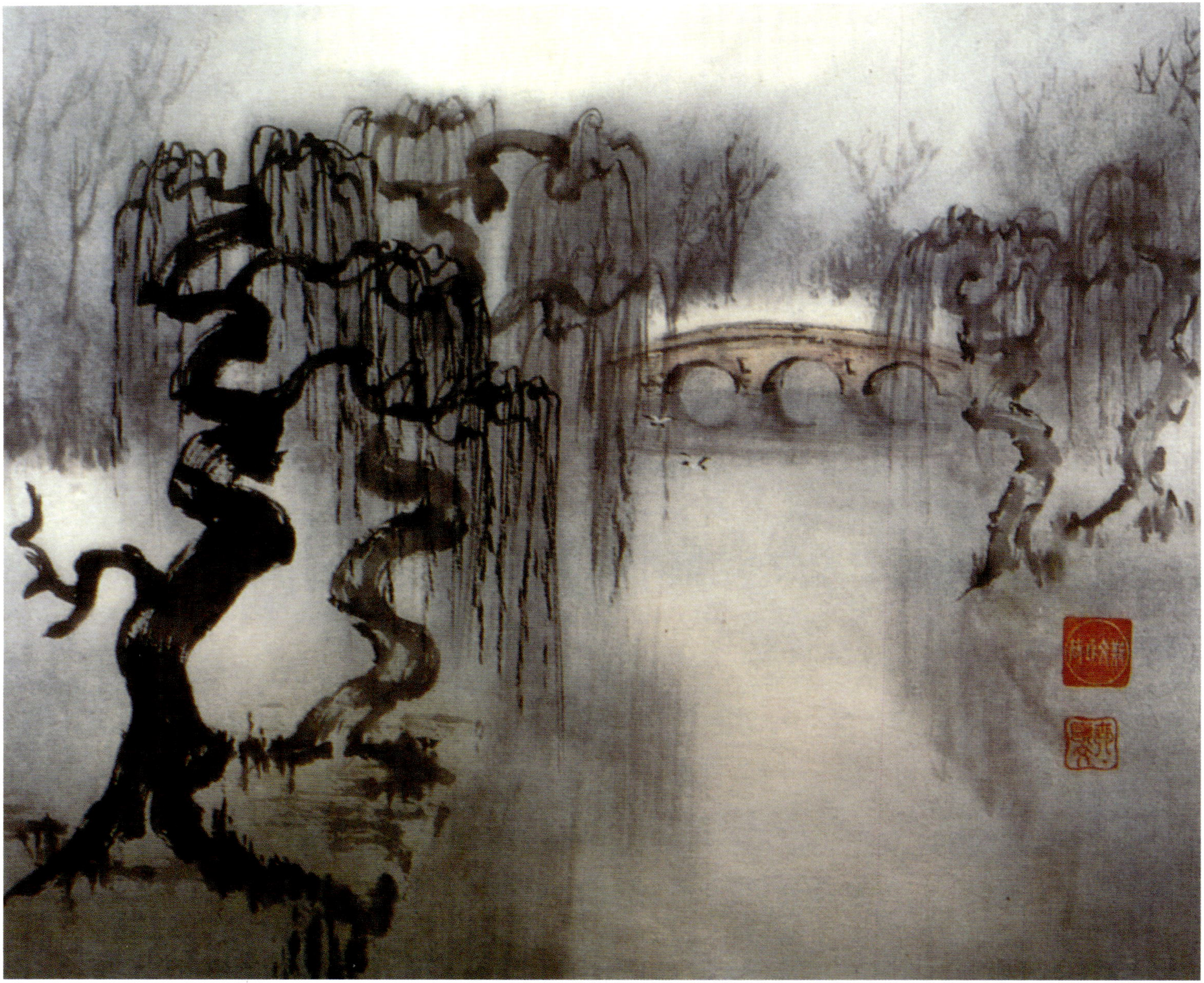

Trinity College Bridge

The willows by the River Cam
appeared to Xu Zhimo,
who would be forever floating
in and out of love,
as young brides all a-glitter
in the river's sunset mirror.

I see slim ladies, in fine gowns,
who could be brides
with their shapely tresses
and sprays of veils;
there's also a three-arched bridge
and two birds all a-flutter
in this Cambridge willow pattern.

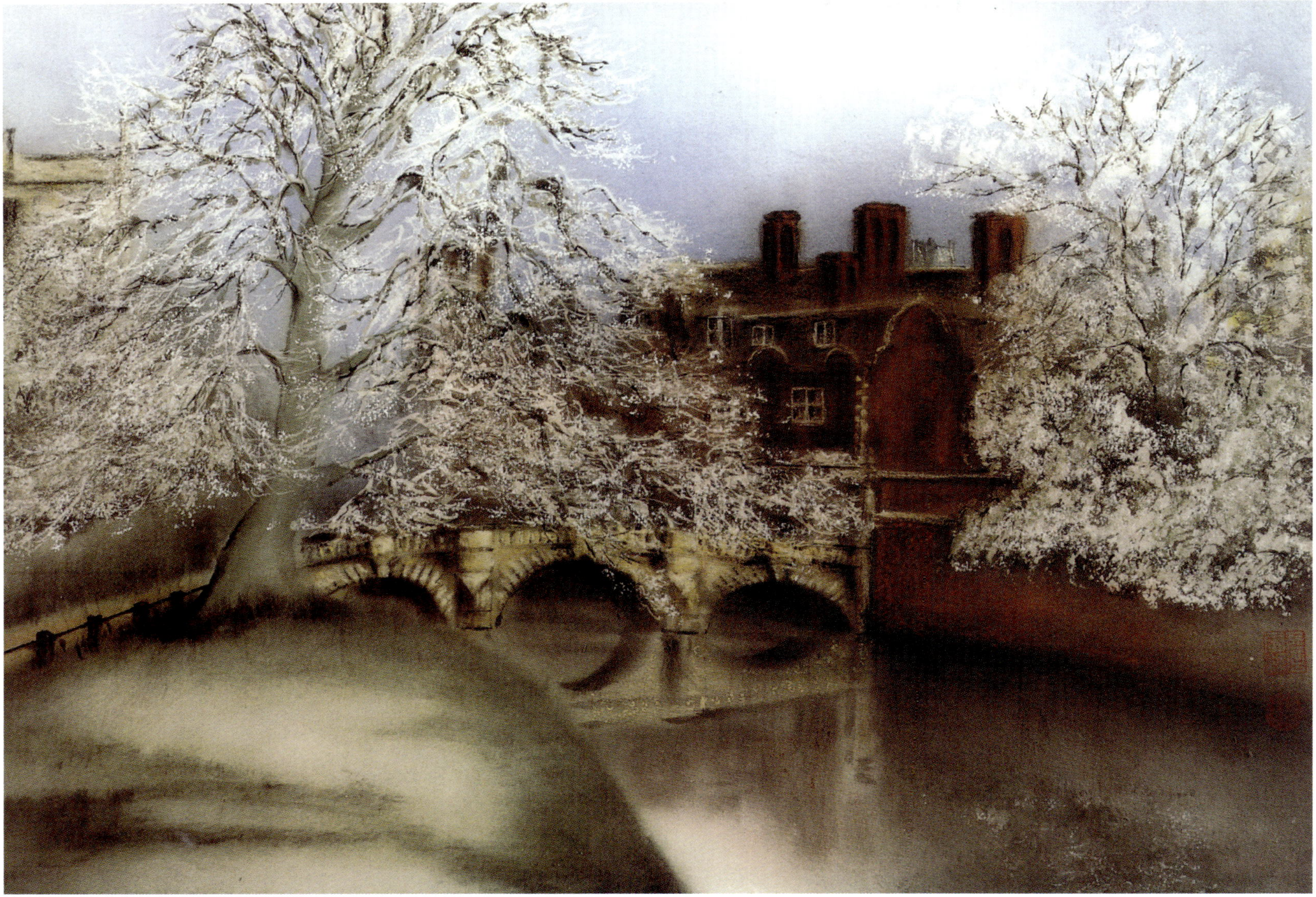

The Cam in Winter

We walked the Backs one winter's day
by lawns of glinting frosted glass,
our feet crunching the gravelled way
that keeps folk like us off the grass.
By the bridge hung a crystal tree
sparkling light above the river,
branches forming a fleur-de-lis –
an ice-sculpted chandelier.
St John's red walls had caught the sun
and I remembered those cold rooms:
First Court, with winter well begun
and just a gas fire's pale blue plumes
over which I hunched, book in hands
trying to ensure I'd join the cast
of next summer's best graduands.

In those free days that couldn't last
the Cam in winter was like this,
calm and empty, no punts on show,
the waters sleeping in deep peace.
But things have changed since then, and now
well wrapped tourists are poled year round;
under the frosty arch comes the prow,
they're snug in rugs, all comforts found.
So I'll look back and think upon
that winter walk beside the Cam
when from blue skies a low sun shone
into a stillness now long gone.

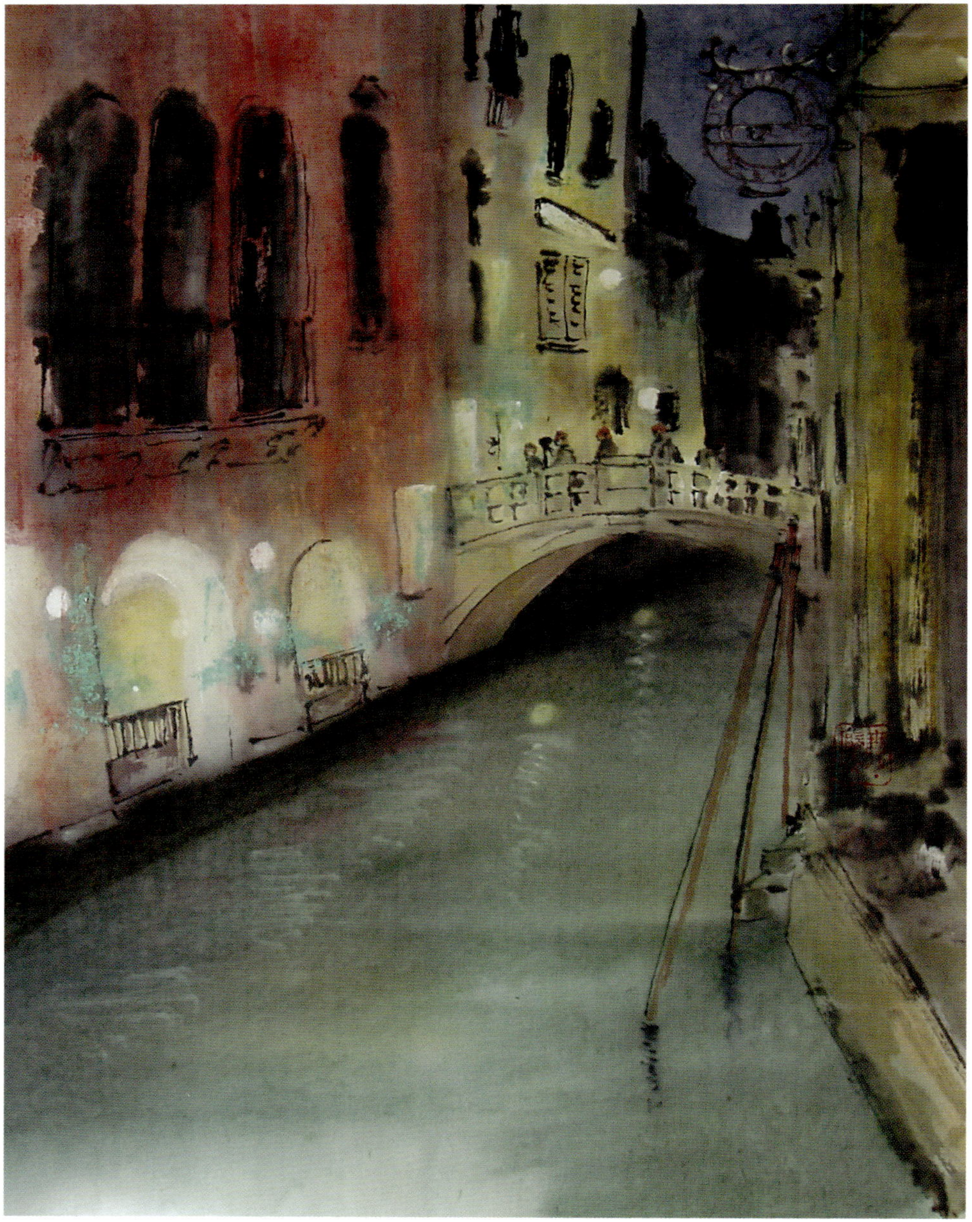

Venice at Night

The night makes blank-eyed cliffs
of empty rooms
hanging lifelessly in shadow,
narrow water streets become
flooded catacombs;
though dead above there's life below
in luminescent pools.

By small canals left off
the guidebook lists,
unremarked by the evening crowd,
are found the quiet places
where Venice exists
and there's no need to shout out loud
like excited herded schools.

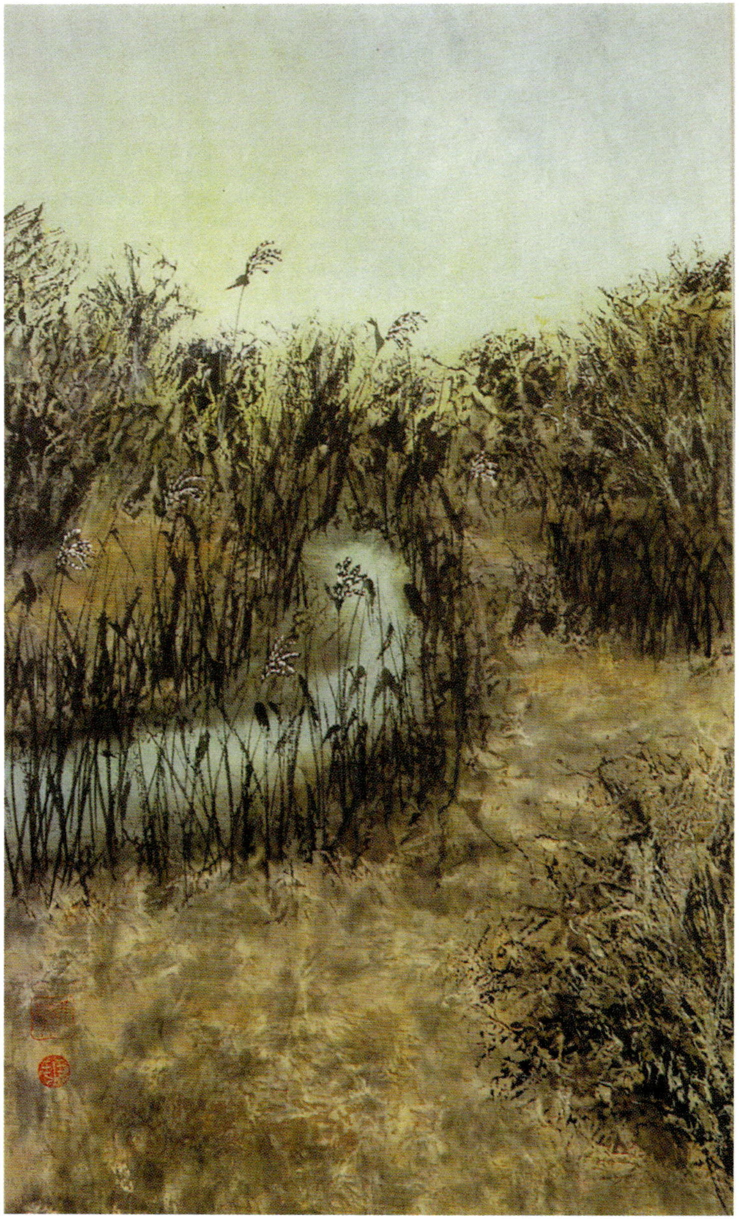

Wicken Fen

Water world woven from sallow and sedge
once reached all the way to the sky's far edge,
then Vermuyden came to conquer the fen;
his Dutchmen attacked, again and again,
slashed long cuts across the country's wet skin,
peeled open the land, bled out what was in.
The world shrivelled down away from the sky,
farms were marked out and we watched the fen die,
its riches taken to grow more to eat;
we kept pecking like crows at the black peat
and gone were the eels, the cranes, dragonflies
that danced in the air to bittern horn cries.

Wicken's wet refuge is guarded by pumps
and ploughs can't disturb sleeping bog oak stumps.
Townsfolk like us drive in cars to come here
to walk by straight lodes once dug to drain mere,
step along boardwalks winding through reed bed,
imagine where Bronze Age causeways once led.
A rustle of rushes, a whirr of wings,
bubbles in the water, all kinds of things
show we've been able to turn back the clock,
persuade banished Nature back to re-stock.
Like pooling raindrops on an opened map,
more schemes like Wicken are filling the gap;
in fifty years it could look like before,
wetland and sky will be our home once more.

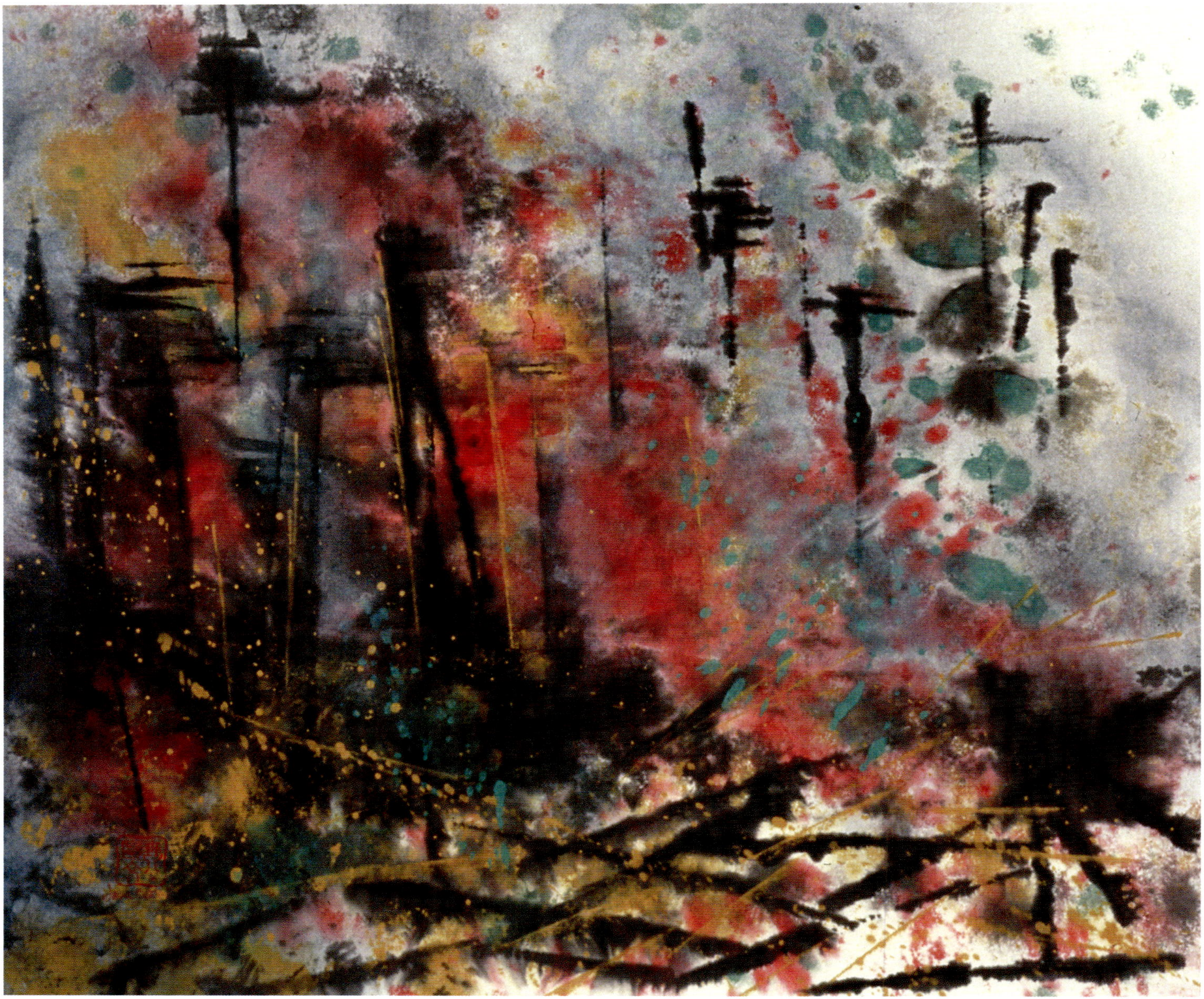

Forest on Fire

Out in the bay, first evening at anchor,
from across the water came a faint roar:
the unearthly calling of insect millions
from the darkening forest that fringed the shore.

Darwin was spellbound in the Bahia woods,
a welcome stroll after landfall at last;
in "… one great wild … luxuriant hothouse …"
his envisioned New World was quite surpassed.

Later, his thoughts went again and again
to where beauty was born of eternal strife
to search once more in that wondrous garden
that held hidden within the clue to life.

Brazil's coastal forest has all but gone,
the frontline of flame is now well inland,
maize marches across vanquished Cerrado,
beef cattle are singed with Amazon brand.

"There's plenty of forest left, what's the gripe?"
but one day we will find that more meant less
like the smokers who shrug, take one more fag
until their lungs become a shrivelled mess.

Green leaves wither,
red flesh chars,
grey smoke chokes,
black bones splinter,
corpses litter;
trees burn at the stake.

Darwin and Wallace each solved the puzzle
and now we know it was all down to chance:
capricious events of natural law
put us here at the top to lead life's dance.
But if we cut off from our common tree
our wilder limbs – mangrove root, monkey hand –
leaving no room for our untamed kin,
then we ourselves will no longer stand.

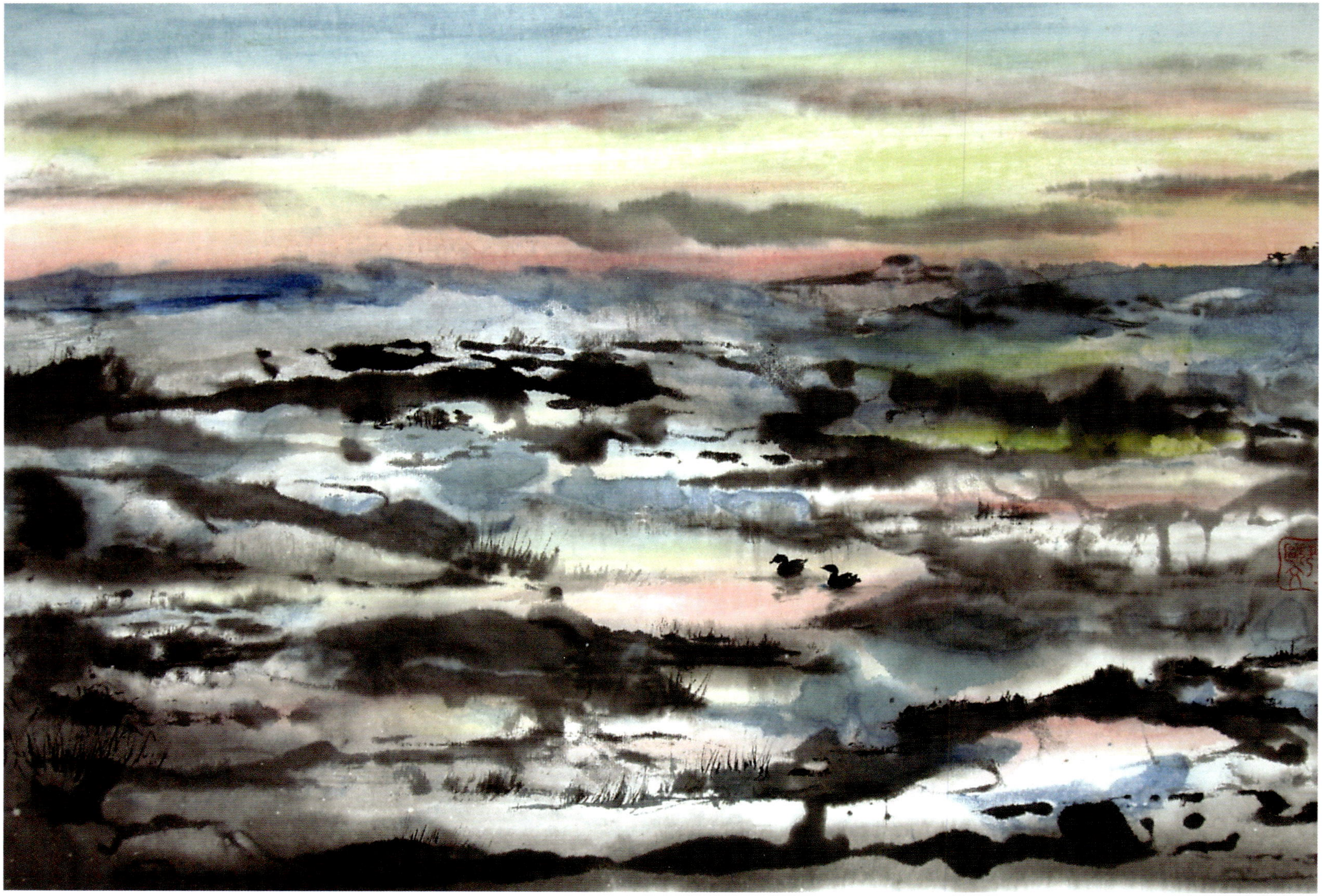

Southwold Marshes

Along the beach we walked one afternoon
by crumbling cliffs retreating from the east.
We set off past a scruffy scrap of marsh,
like the grey sea of no note in the least.

Onwards we went, skirting some concrete blocks
dropped there one time to push the sea away;
then, getting late, we turned, came crunching back
over pebbles lit by a sky less grey.

Our friends ahead, who lived here, didn't see
us stop amazed back by the boggy site,
to marvel at the oily pools on fire –
all licking flames of golds and reds alight.

And we wondered, standing to face the glow
of a vast sky burning across the west,
did these ducks afloat on liquid silver
see what we saw – Nature's art at its best?

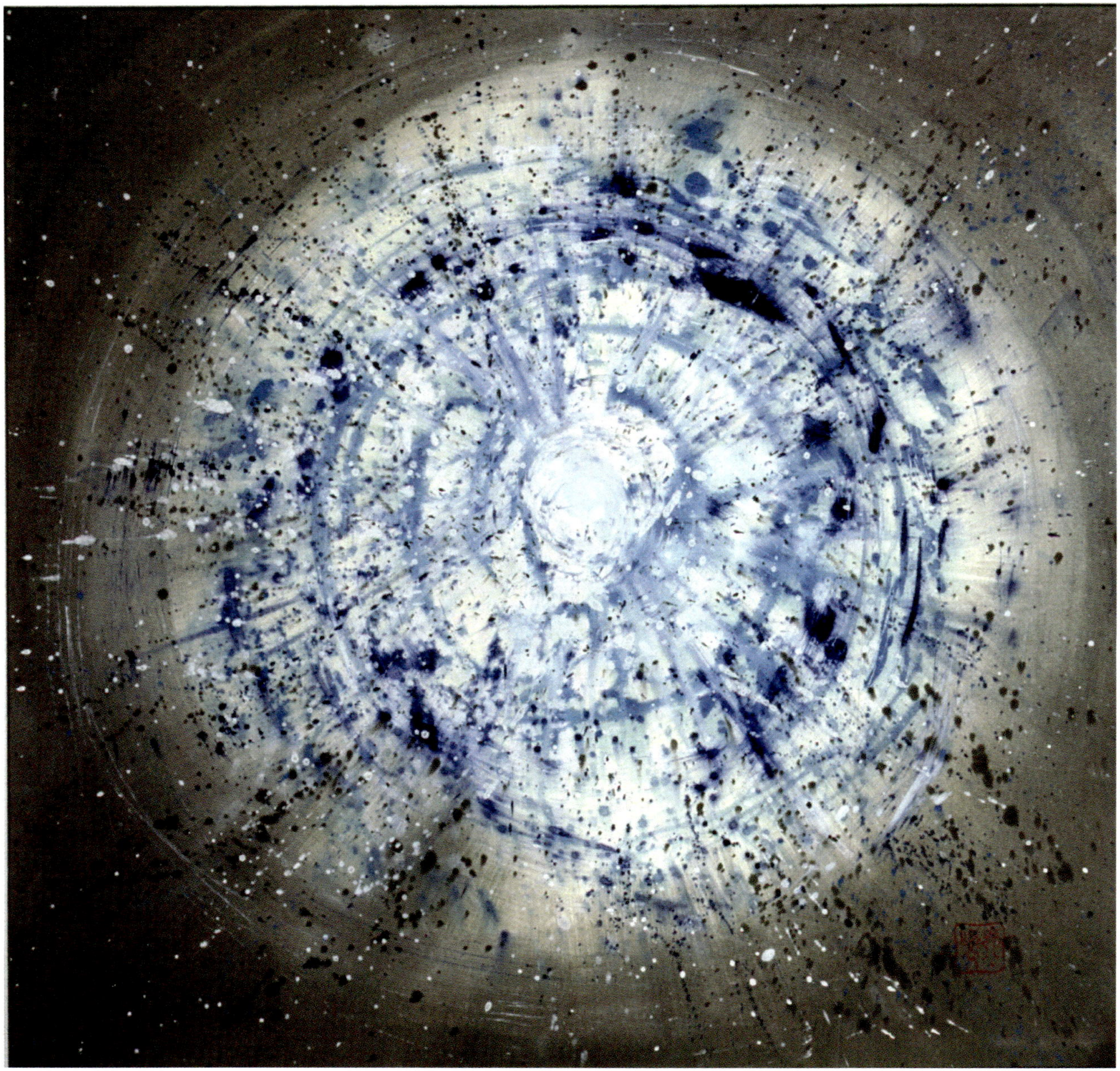

Il Duomo

We pause …
to whisper in huddles
beneath the infinite weight
of soaring stone and crowning marble;
then we step forward,
lift our eyes
and are bathed
in the sudden sunburst
of Filippo's miracle

that turns us
into bubbles of air
floating up to the light
encircled by angels and saints
as the heavens' blue skies
pour down inside
mixing time and space
in the dazzling explosion
of the power and the glory
that is the Universe,
its end and its beginning.

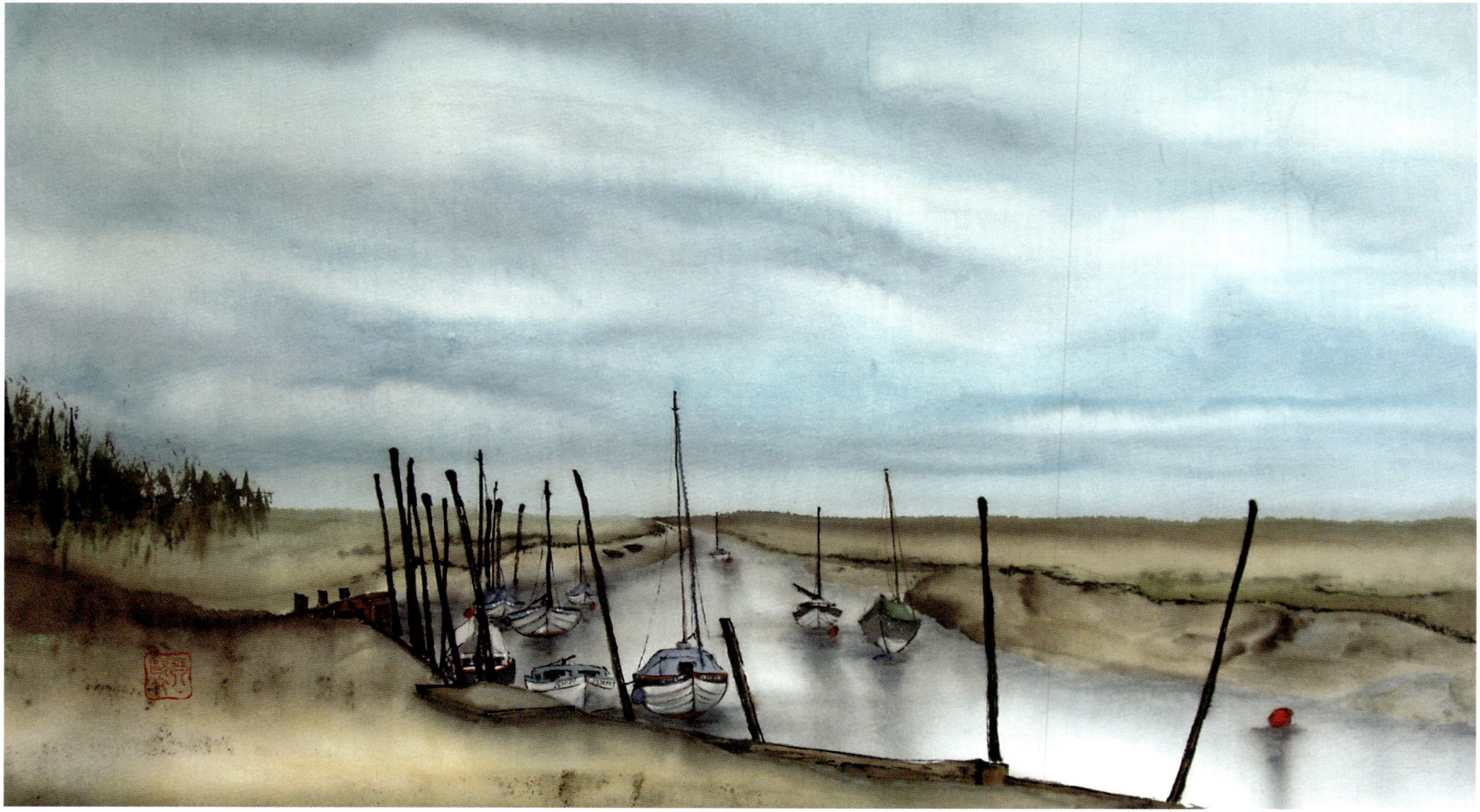

At anchor

It's easy to believe
in a flat earth
here, on the endless levels
at the world's edge, where
England's bold coastline
loses its way
to wander aimlessly
along coils of creeks
in a salt marsh maze
that's neither land nor sea
and goes on for ever;
masts and mooring posts
the only pins in a map
of where water is,
for the moment,
anchored to the land.

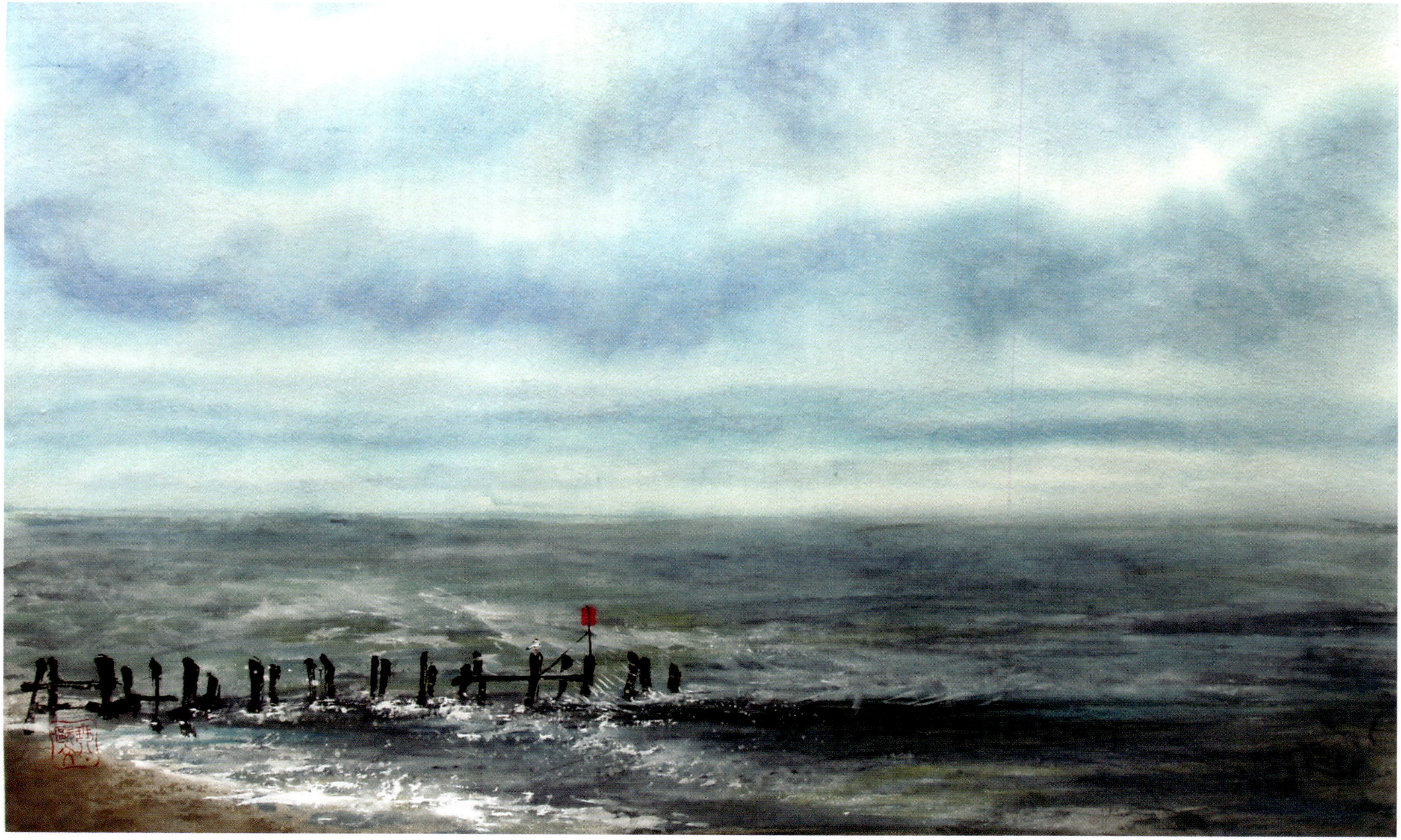

Groyne at Southwold

We march in pairs into the sea
behind our flag for all to see,
water salting our shining boots
we'll nail the shingle with these roots.

It may have pulled Dogger under
but these shores are not for plunder;
we'll hold the line of England's east:
no more land lost to this beast.

Cliffs may tumble and houses fall
but we'll stay brave and stand up tall;
we'll all go down tied to our mast
our colours flying to the last.

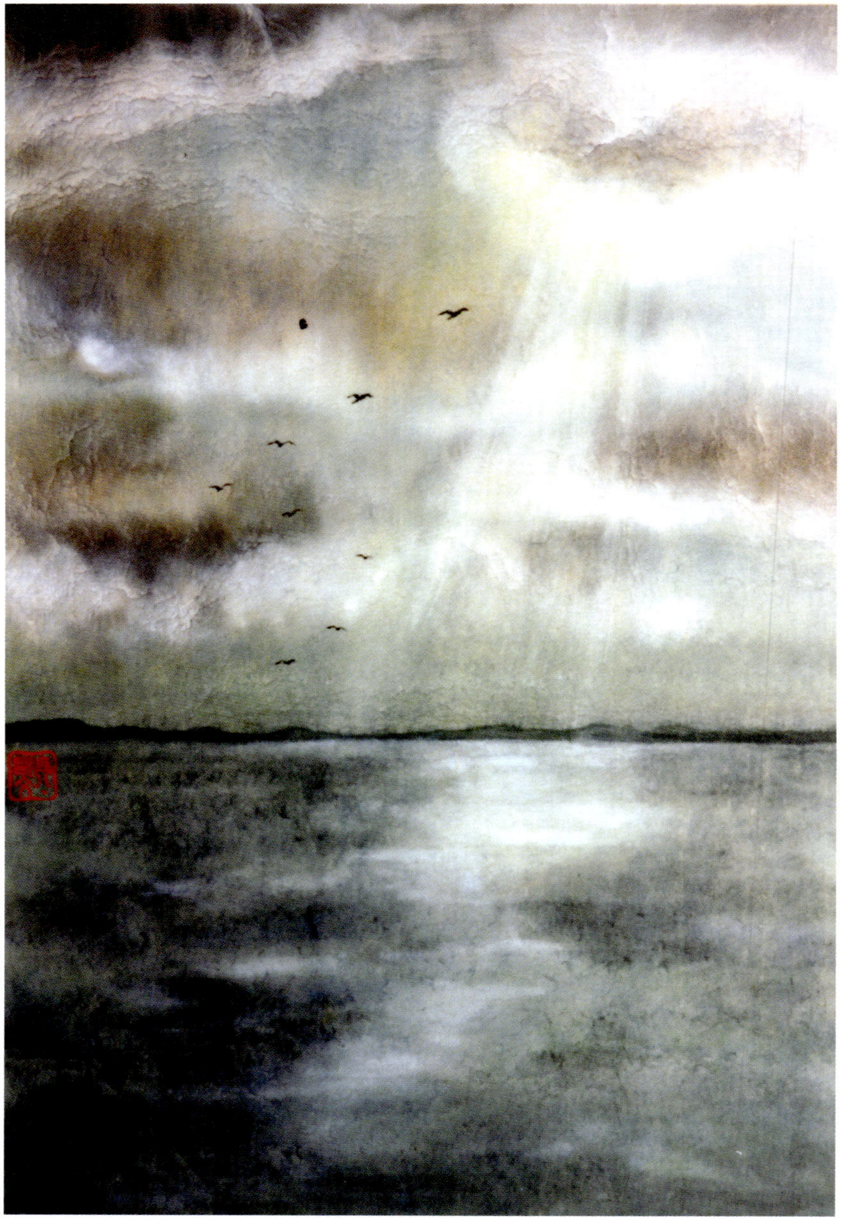

Storm Brewing in the Channel

They were bluer skies and lighter seas
for sun bright starts to summer holidays;
out on throbbing deck to feel the breeze
and almost touch huge gulls in their displays
of hanging so still in warm diesel air
before wheeling away to check the wake
but with us all the way from here to there.
Oh, what good memories those crossings make.

Then we saw the sky begin to darken,
angry clouds blew up and came rolling in;
deep currents had stirred to wake the kraken
that can only see foes in those not kin;
it blindly roared from white Dover cliffs
that we're an island and must cut these ties
for they all gang up to do us mischief.
Its foul breath rose up and blacked out the skies.

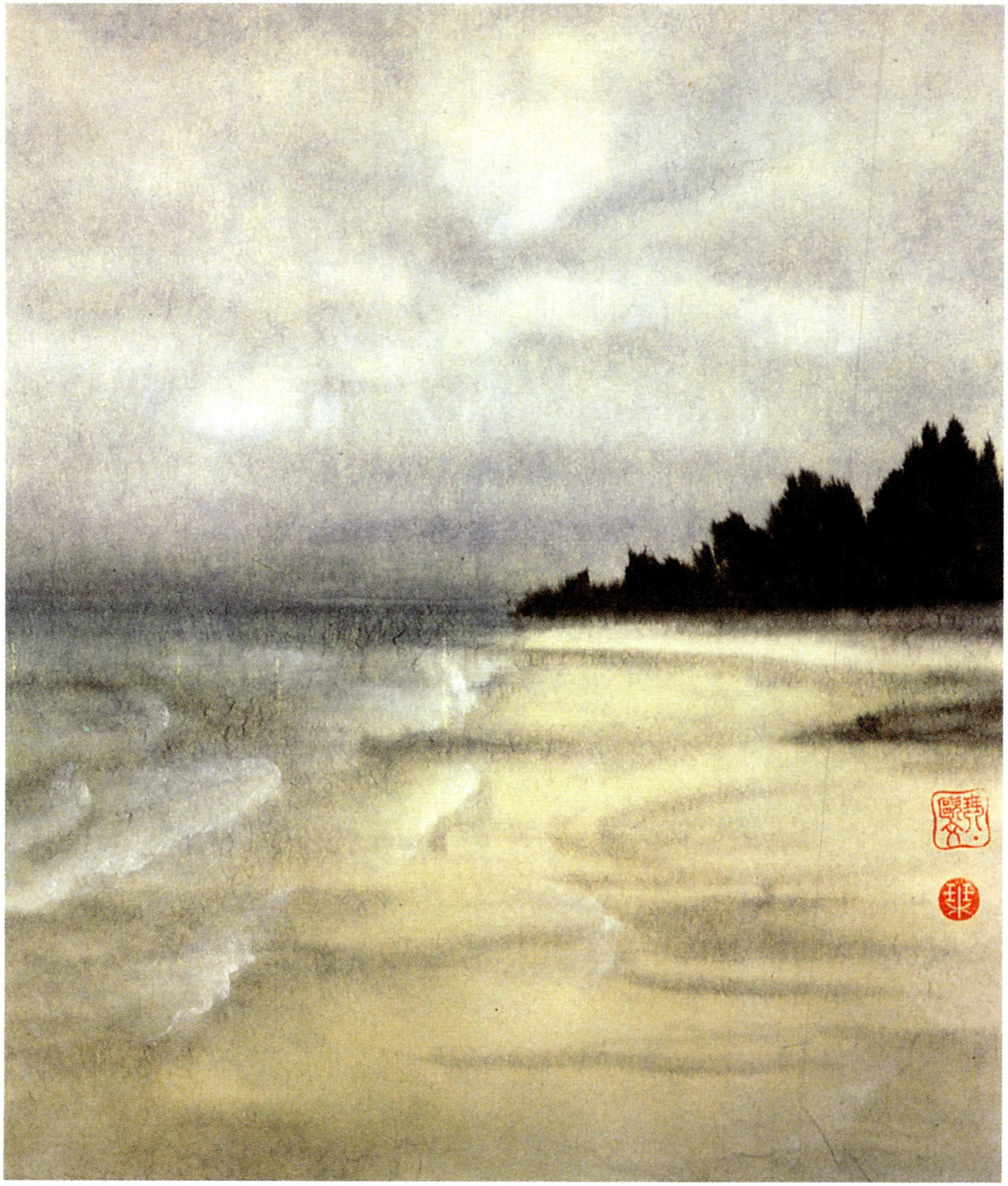

Diani Beach

Long, long Diani Beach
footprint-free for miles,
the leaden overcast that day
lightened by the children's smiles
as they felt the bath-warm water
come rippling over their feet
and the line of watching palm trees
seemed to be waving in the heat;
then plucking up new scoops of beach
to squeeze them through their hands,
they built an outpost in this place
in towers of dripping sand.

They'd gone next day, the world refreshed
by the timeless wash of the sea;
our forebears, though, were less content
to leave no legacy.
We'd come last time with loaded guns,
now we bring our snorkeling gear,
crossing half the globe again
for a tropical sundown beer.

At hotel reception later
was a tourist in loud complaint:
because of rain that morning
he hadn't been able to paint;
I was alright, knew about things,
as I was in Kenya to work
– thought of helping the manager,
perhaps nod a knowing smirk –
instead I raised an eyebrow
and offered worldly sympathy
but he had learned the hard way
the trap of conspiracy.
"The weather's not my fault", he said,
straight into the eye of the storm
and rain man swept off, red of face
in darkly thunderous form;
the manager then turned away
leaving the sadder thought with me
that he hadn't felt he could trust me
when I stayed with him by the sea.

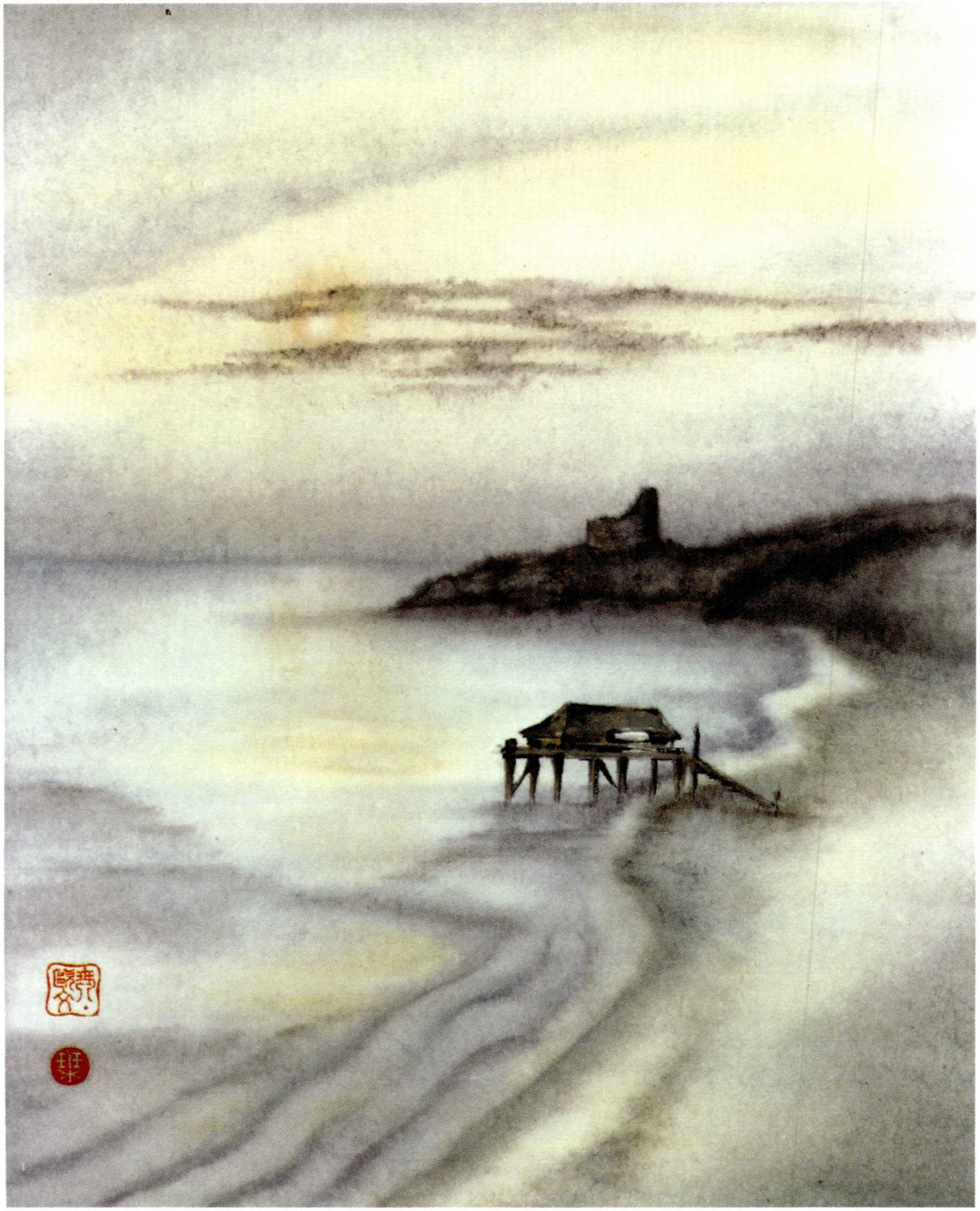

Near Anzio

It's afternoon in spring
and the sun has tired of the day,
using what's left of the heat
to fuse sea and sky together
and veil its slow retreat.

Mid-week, out of season,
hotels and restaurants closed now,
hardly anyone around.
Biding its time, the sea comes to
recover its lost ground.

It licks the beach with care
and with each exploring ripple,
grain by grain dissolves the sand
and, blushing a little, takes the
last colour off the land.

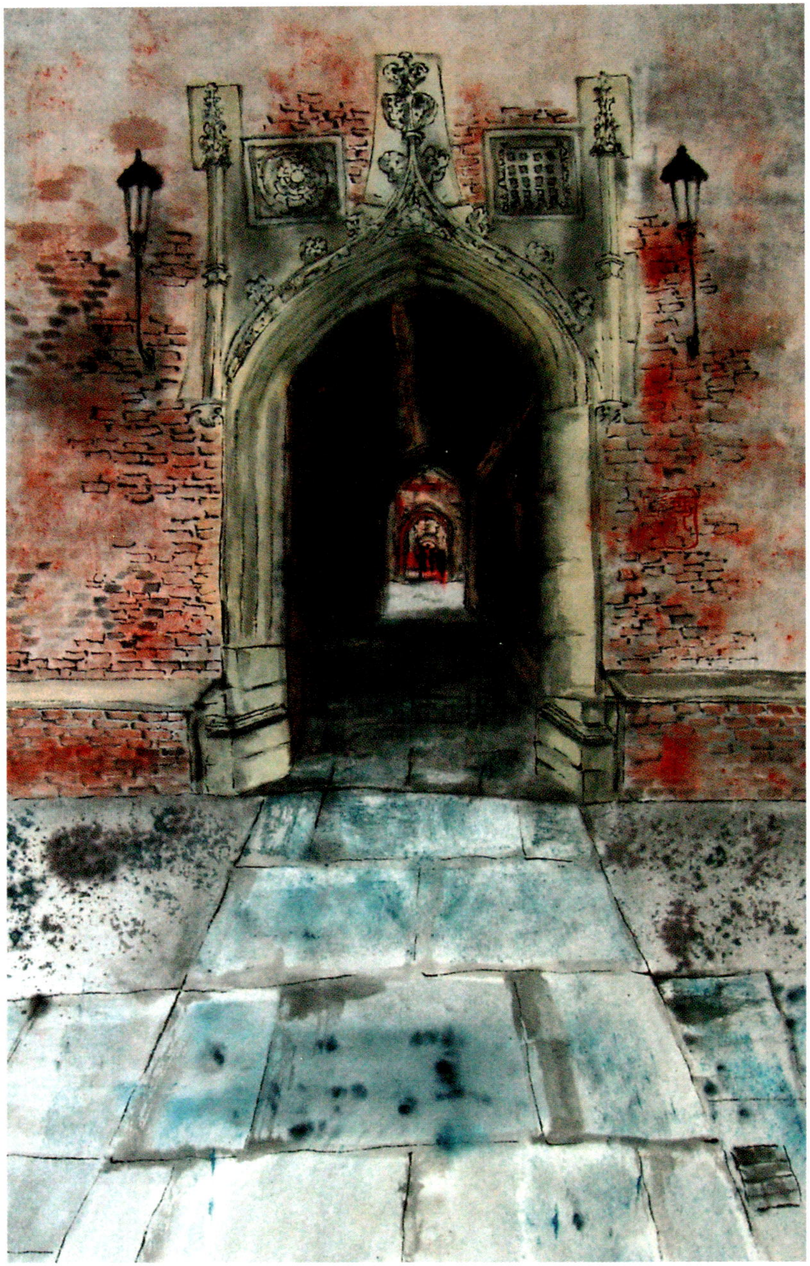

St John's College Portal

It was hard to get into this poem
as it's hard to go through this arch
and feel it belongs to you as much as
to all the scholars who have marched
in procession a half millennium,
but for our easy casualness
of grimy gowns and rude entry through tall
wooden doors to gilded
splendour in the high hallowed hall.
Long Latin grace then the clamour
of earnest diners and well-fed prophets,
until those with backs to the walls
step onto the monkish tables and leave;
never so sure was privilege.

Beneath Margaret Beaufort's proud portcullis
and King Henry's uniting rose,
walk through here into St John's Tudor heart
where every brick is cherished
and feel the strong pumping of beating thoughts
of what we know and need to find.
As we follow those who have searched before
each court crossed leads to another beyond,
each door opened shows one more door;
within this maze of learning few abscond,
most carry with them throughout life
that slice of time when they went through this gate
to eat, to pray, to work, to play
and armoured thus seek out their fate.

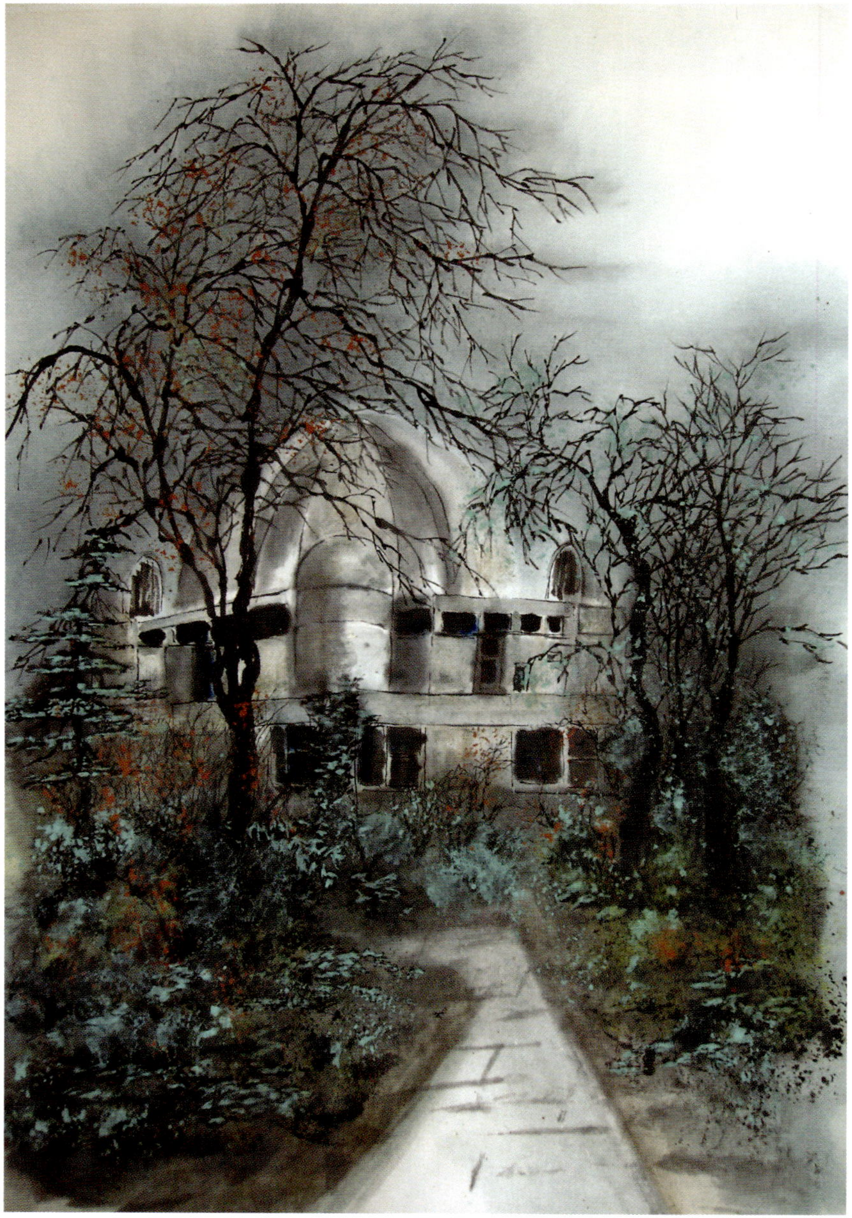

New Hall

My mother's Cambridge degree
was thought less worthy;
she was female
and so had to wait a lifetime
before heavy wrong was lightly righted
and the long-dead scroll placed at last,
with just sufficient ceremony,
in her forgiving arthritic hand
– the one that didn't hold the stick.

All hail, then
to the temple of the sky,
brave dome rising
from earthly gardens,
monument of the mind
fortified against unbelievers,
high challenge to fusty cloisters
where tired ideas inbred
a fool's blindness
to half the world's riches.

A new reactor core
to alchemise rare brilliance
from metal dismissed as base;
an observatory, doors
confidently sliding back,
to uncover other worlds.

In time, all will come here
to learn;
just you see.

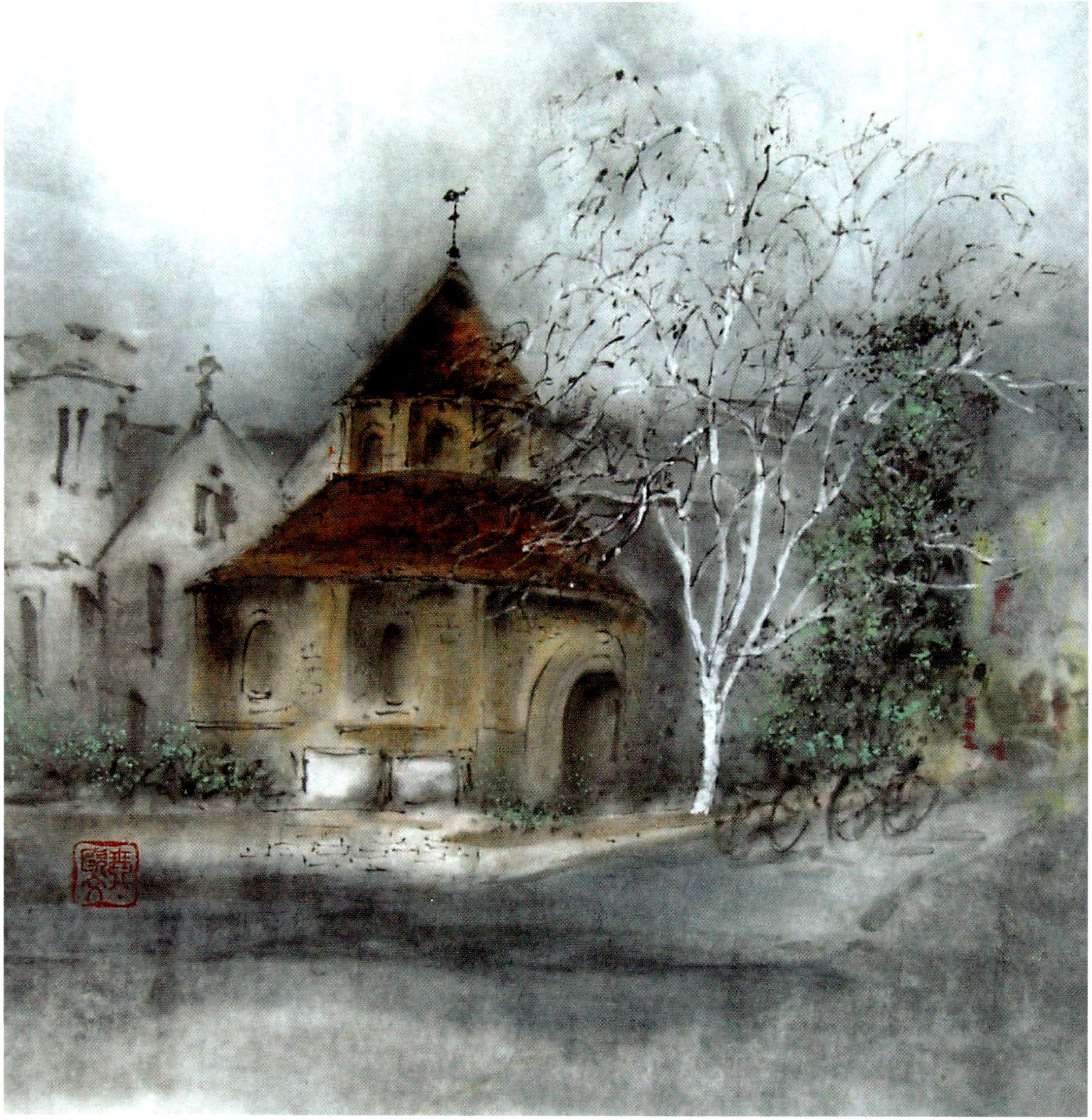

The Round Church

Like a lantern set down
under John's dark frown,
it's chubby, mascot sized,
and squats on the ground
but the inside belies
with arches and pillars
in close double rings:
a hint of the Levant
this ancient place brings.
Sooner or later
everybody goes past:
returning to a car park
from the middle of town
or late for lectures and
pedalling fast down
past Trinity and John's
or heading for the river
and the punts by the bridge.

It's somewhere to meet
or buy the Big Issue,
its wall is for sitting
or re-tying a shoe
or propping cycles
to leave for a while.
It's a favourite for selfies
with a tourist's smile;
it seems the whole world
knows this odd little church.

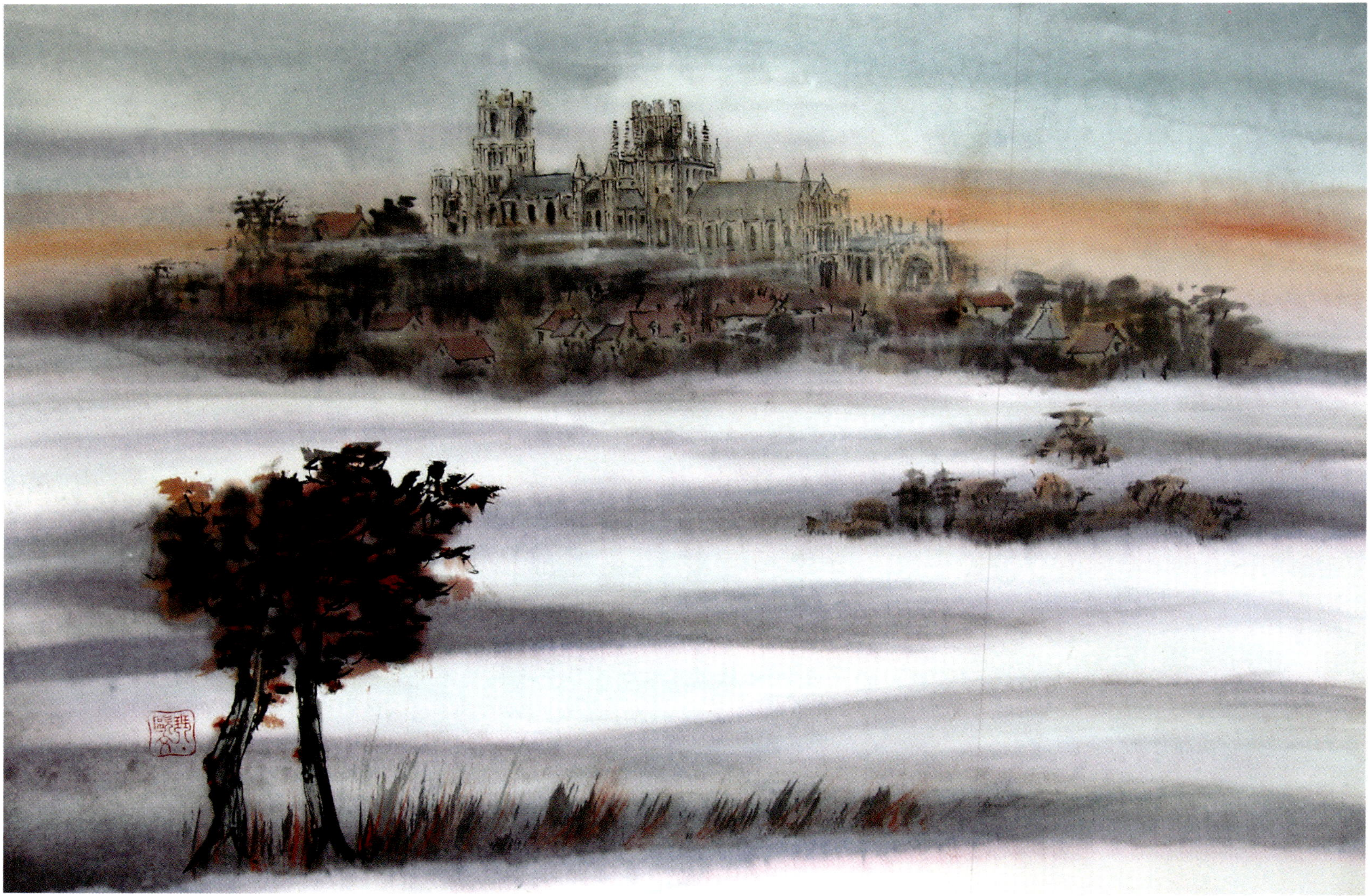

Ely Cathedral

God's ship of stone dry-docked on its island,
proudly hull high in the morning sky;
its octagon lantern astride the plain
stretching sea wide on every side.

On this uprising Hereward stood,
held off William's men across marsh and fen,
then traitors' footsteps picked out the path
and out of the mists came chain mailed fists.

Ely huddles to save and be saved,
to lift up to heaven its saints again;
loose this shrine from its earthly moorings,
let Æthelthryth ride with the sky's high tide.

Towering landmark for a thousand years,
its pilgrim profile is seen from miles;
adrift from Cambridge, halfway to the sea,
all our story lies there in Ely.

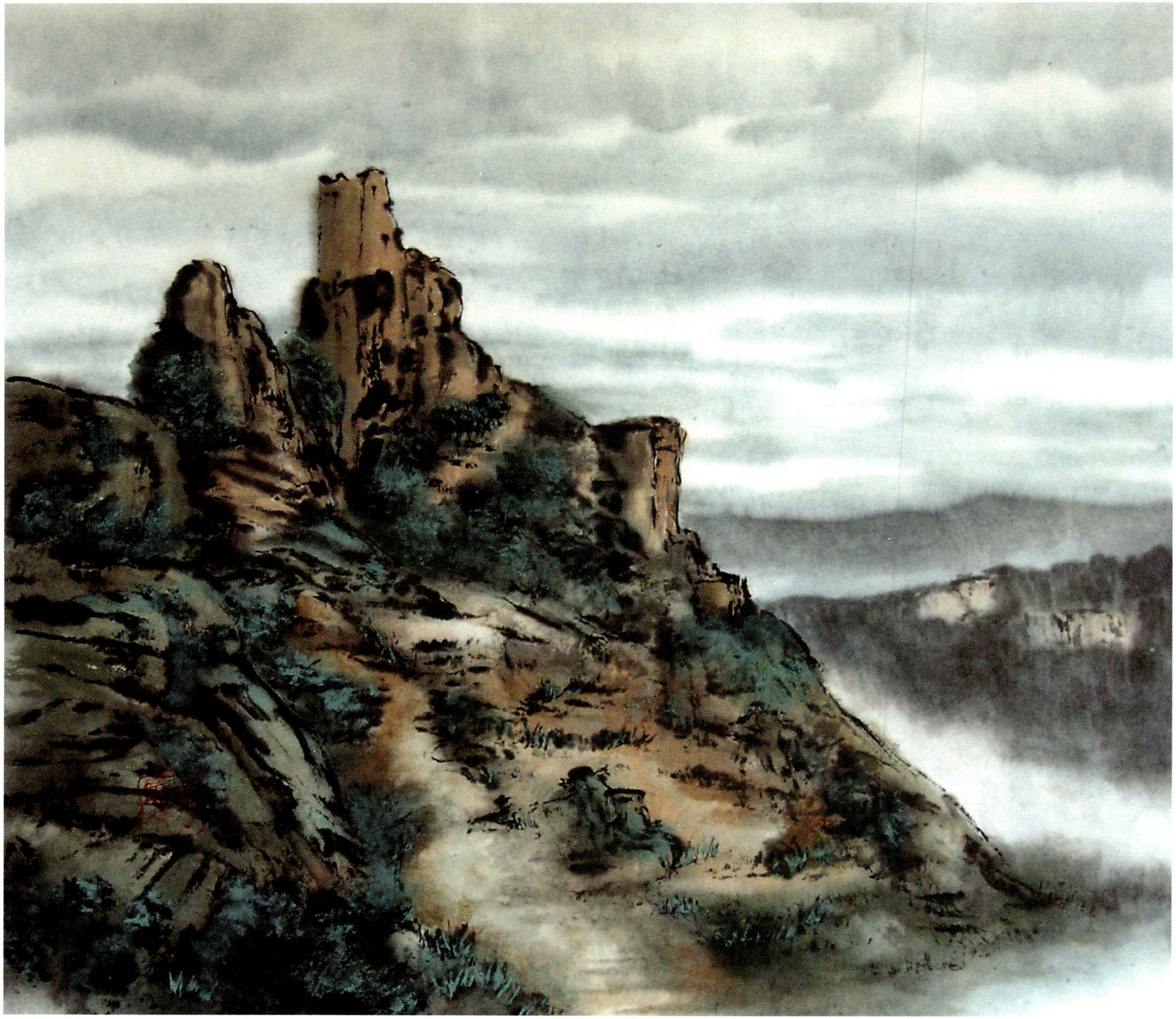

Rochebonne

We will be safe
if we build
on this rock
hanging high
above the valley.
We will put up with
winter winds
blowing smoke back
into cold rooms
of hard faced stone
and clinging mists
forever dampening
clothes and bedding
for we will see
and hear them
far below
long before they
can reach us
and their arrows
and slingshots
start striking our walls
while we scan
the distant ridges
for glints of armour
and flights of pennants
and get ready
to welcome
victorious friends
or fight off
strengthened foes.

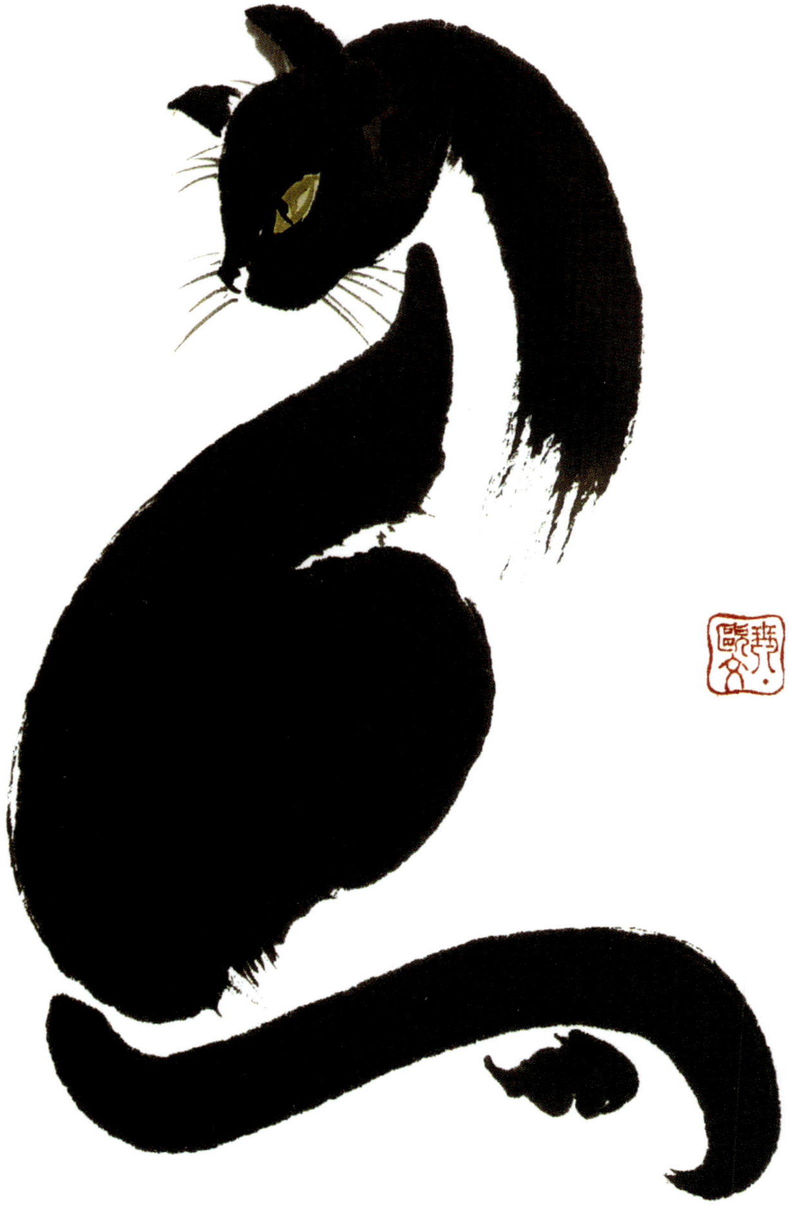

Cat

Each step thought out
Deliberately
Picked and placed precisely
Now stopped poised
Head turned held still
To watch to listen
Two bodies in one
Relaxed
Sleek curves basking
Staying put in the sun
Taut
Wound-up snake-tail spring
Primed to strike
Black or white
Half there half not there
A Schrödinger cat
Crystallised disdain for eyes
You may admire me
But keep your distance.

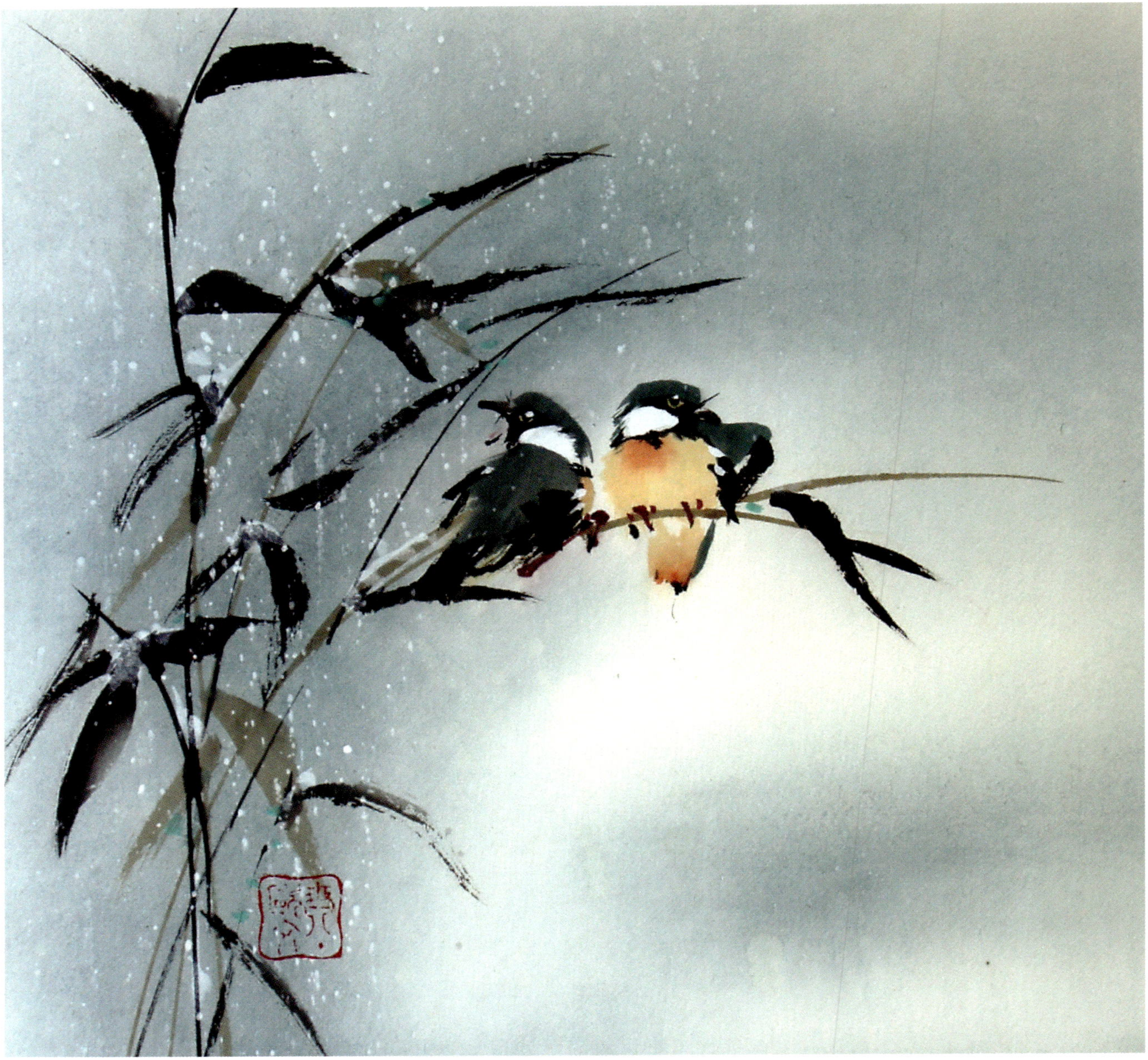

Two's Company … ?

Leaden stillness
snow falling softly
settling carefully
bamboo spearheads
slowly lowered.

Stem bobbing gently
featherweight perching
second bird joining
looking around
almost touching.

Lingering on
or about to leave
will one go
and the other stay
or both go off together?

They've vanished
stem lifting slightly
snow falling softly
leaden stillness
were they really here?

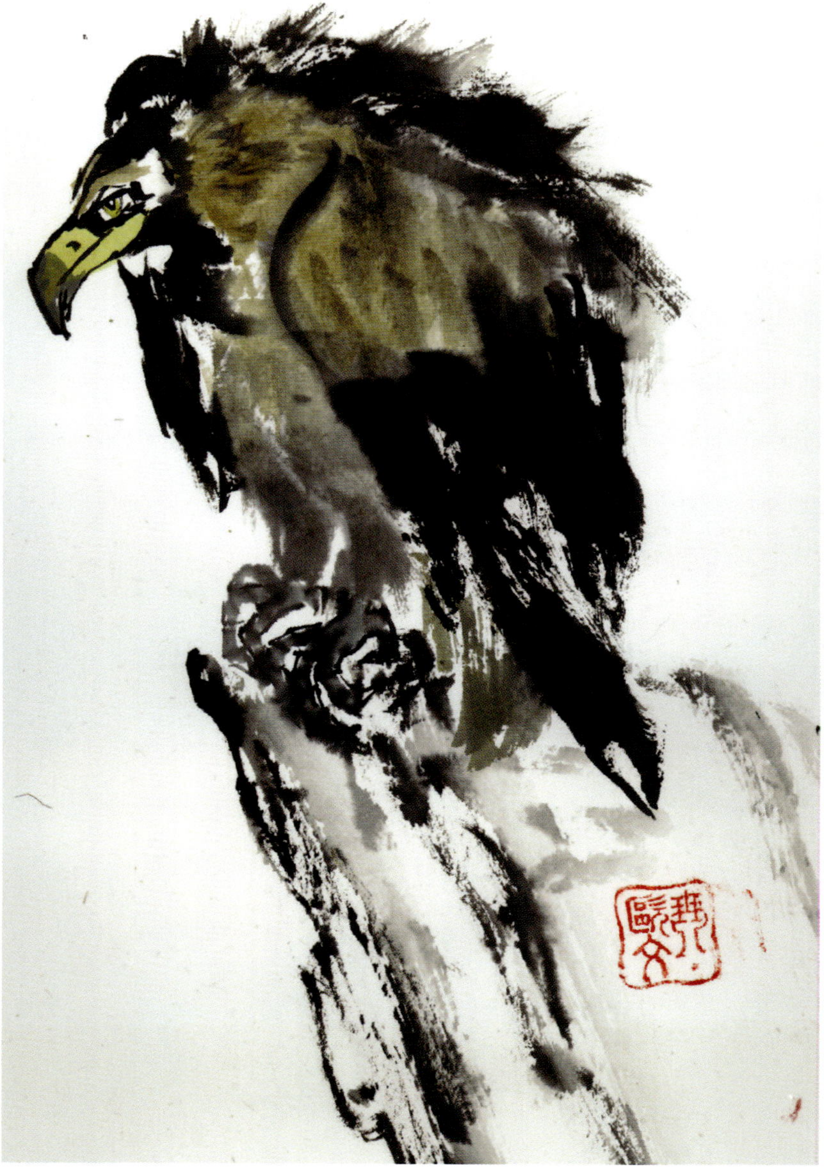

Eagle

Yes, you're right, I am an eagle
and I don't like this sodding rain
any more I guess than you do,
if you'll excuse my crude refrain.

I'm trying to dry my feathers
up on this windy lump of rock;
I know I don't look fierce enough
and so I'll thank you not to mock.

The proud bird of choice I may be
for many coats of arms worldwide,
but you don't feel very royal
when you're miserable inside.

I'm not getting any younger,
find it harder to catch the prey
and also look imperial -
be an eagle every day.

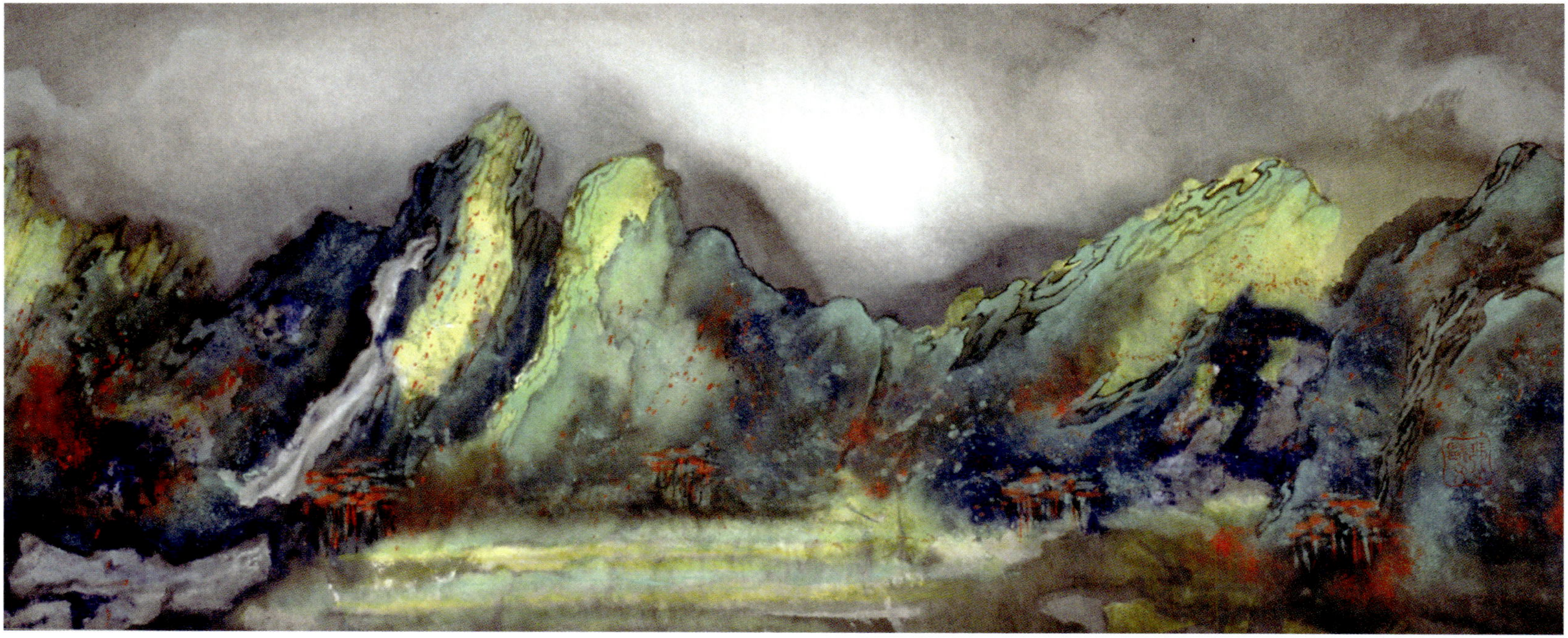

Mountains of the Mind

What did you see,
you who have beheld these ranges
from behind closed eyes?

Stacked slices of geological cake
cut deeply from layers of time,
a rainbow wall, which if you devoured it,
would bring you fame for evermore;
so you camped that night on the plain below,
chose your route for the next day's climb
but when dawn's light came, you found you
couldn't move?

You already stood on that ghastly ridge
crushed by the weight of the mountains
and about to fall (oh, how many times!)
off the sheer drop to the blackness below
to find again, as G. M. H. had known,
the abyss where the black dogs wait
becomes each time more bottomless
than before?

An other world in the farthest reach
of the universe, place of exile
where incandescent meteors burned
holes in black storms of noxious gases
and an endless rain drummed inside your skull
as you hid in cracks among the rocks
and counted your frightful loneliness
in light years?

Wondrous peaks of glistening gold,
divine light behind parting clouds,
lush fields, ripe trees, a waterfall,
a Garden of Eden, a Shangri-La;
your land of peace and harmony
where all was good, life eternal
and you hoped, so hoped, it could be
found again?

What mountains did you see in
your mind's eye?

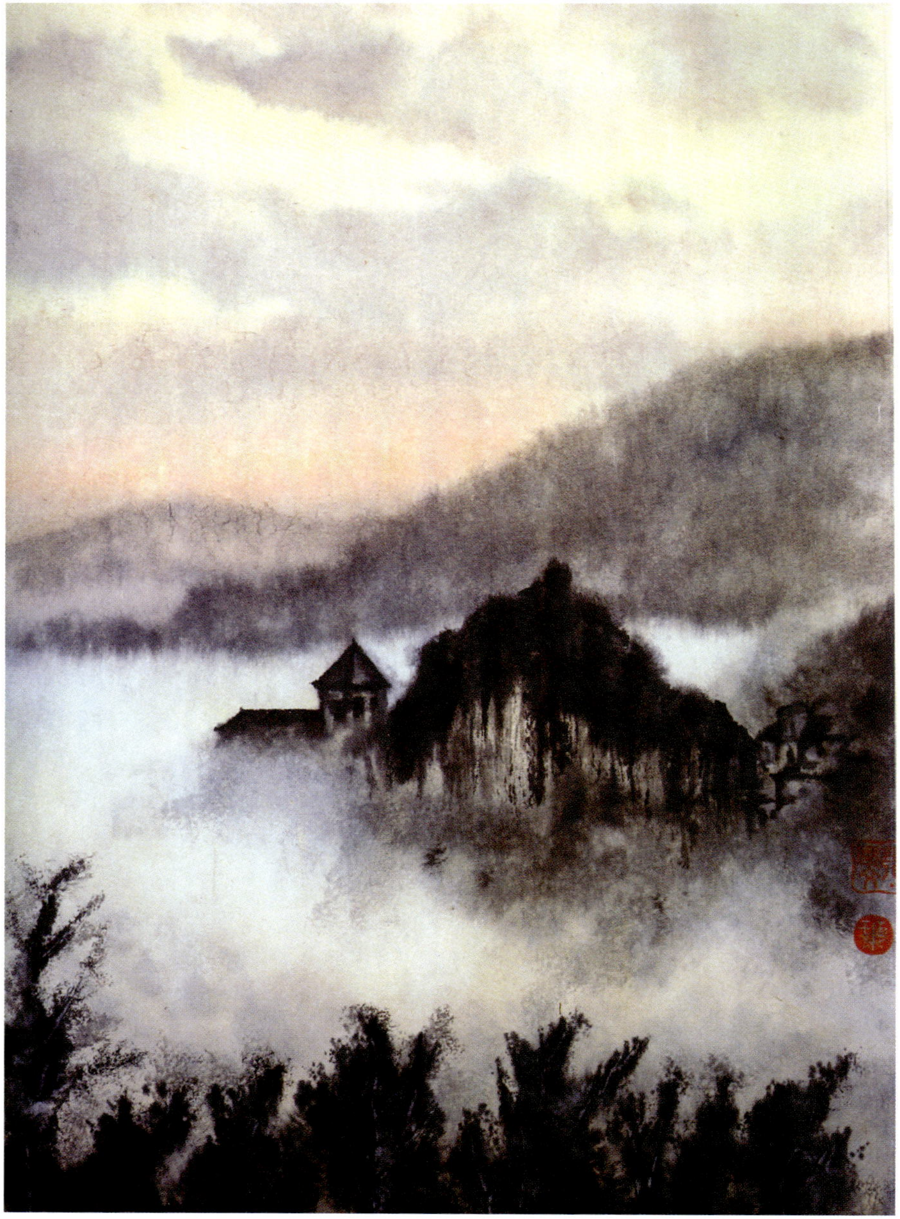

Saint-Cirq-Lapopie

In old China, the highest art
was to paint a landscape,
the works of mortal men
being minor adornments
for the finest fabric
of plunging gorges, soaring crags
and mist-white garlands
of gossamer clouds.

Here, St Cyr's hanging church
peeps over the shoulder
of a mighty rock, bathed
in steaming air below;
above, there is a sky
in imperial golds and reds
between heaven and earth,
joining East with West.

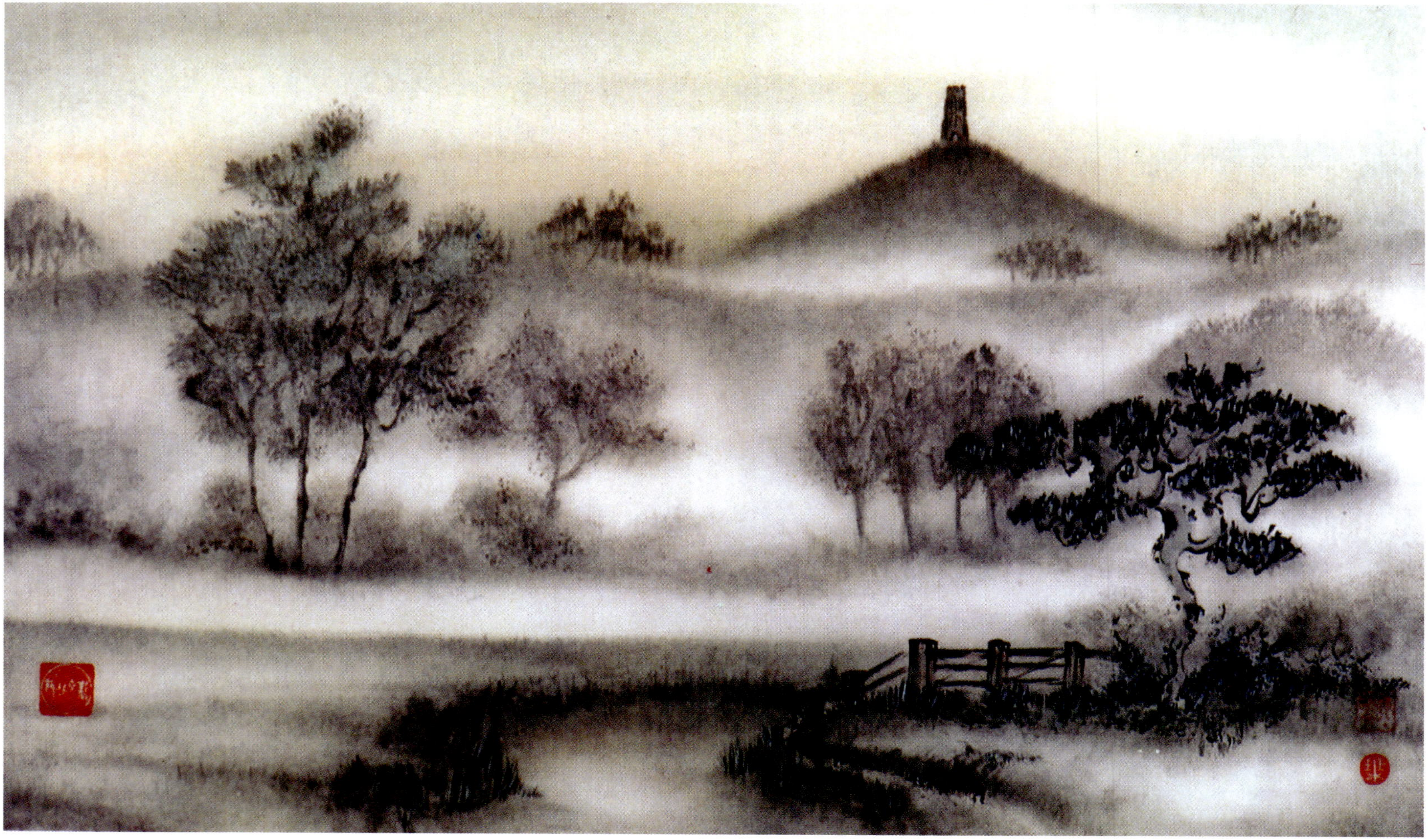

Glastonbury Tor

Streaked drops of dawn's first light
slyly blood the ditch's glass,
first hint that night's white sheets,
laid heavily on the Levels,
will be drawn away
by coming day's damp fingers
and these ancient wetlands
will give up their ghosts of trees again.

We wander across the fields of mist
until the tower traps our eye,
commanding us to see its empty stone
staring sightlessly from on top
of this strange hill heap
where dead monks once swung;
but saying nothing,
silent for centuries.

This won't do
and we demand some meaning -
an enigma at the least -
to entertain our silly modern minds:
it's Arthur's Island of Avalon
or where Celtic Lords of Otherworld once dwelt
or the crystal centre-knot
of all old England's zodiac lines!

Leave it alone,
it has nothing more to say
about far-off long-ago;
let the tower on its tor
sink back into the bogs below
and haunt us no more.

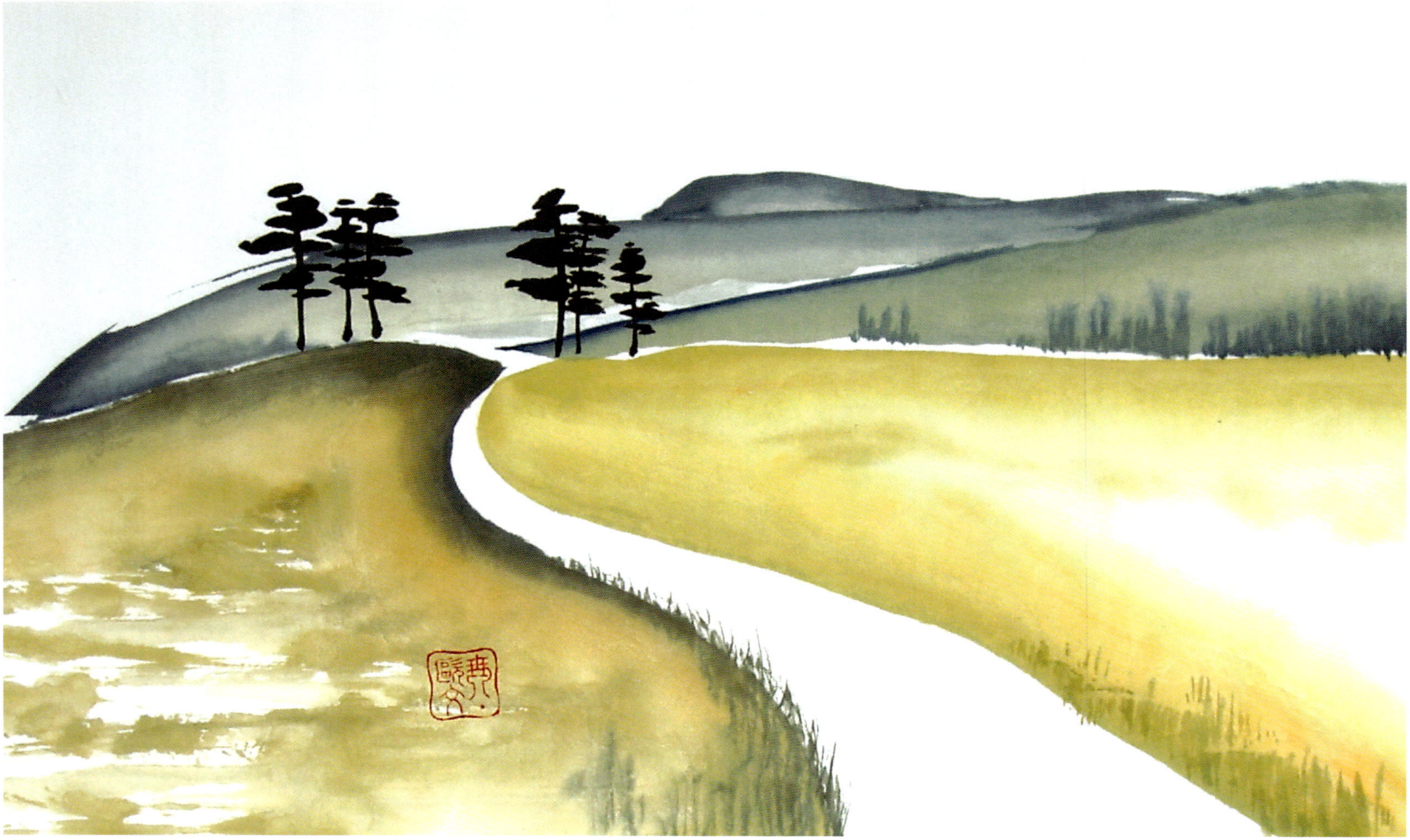

Le Lisieux

The bare boss of Lisieux stone
compasses our small world
capping every skyline here
bolting down our mountain shield
compressing our land
in a million year old grip.

Lest the bubbling and boiling
should come again,
earth's fiery bowels uncoil
and molten guts come snaking up
Lisieux's burning throat
to be heaved out in blistering fluxes
of black-hot liquid rock.

Long since cooled and hard cast
into new rolls of hills
whose dead earth skins
softened with rain and winter ice
bleached with sun
began to live and sprout again
put on a forest coat and make
green the solid seascape
on which we now float.

A few light strokes
will quietly catch
the sweeps and heaps
and gently mingling shades
in a single breath.

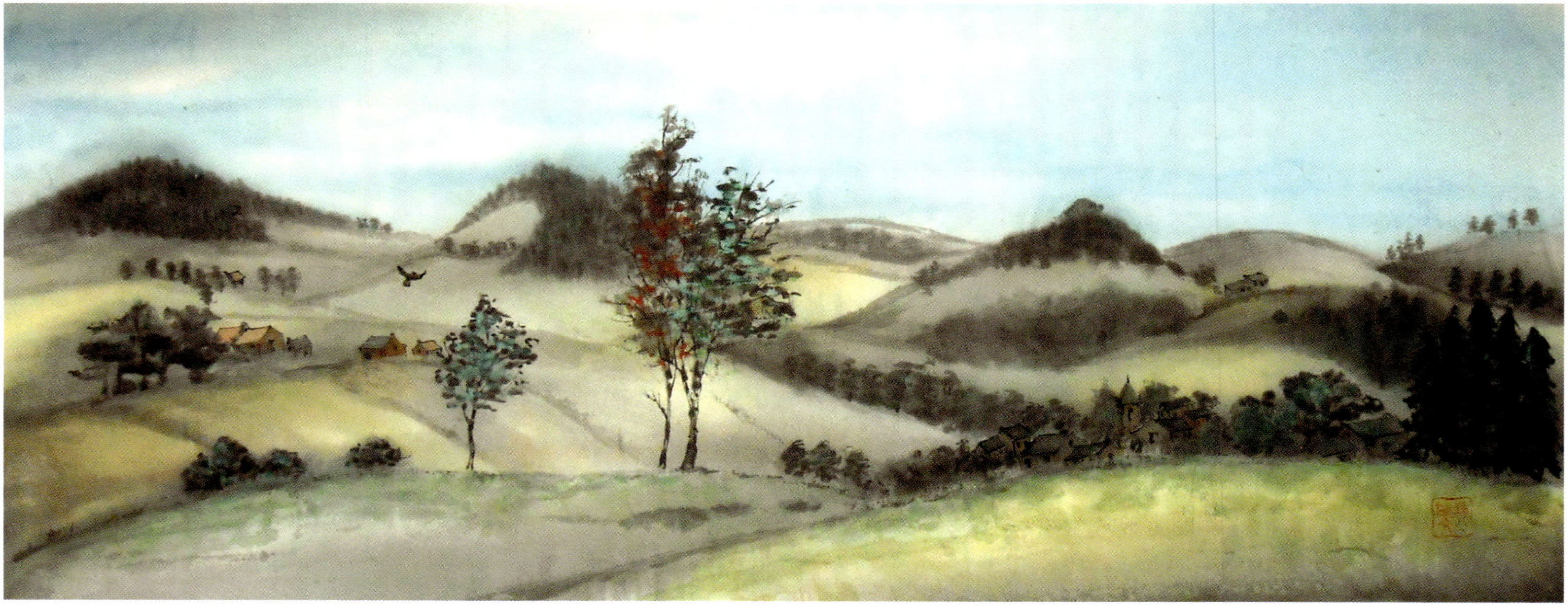

Valley of the Auze

Solid waves roll south from our door
and swell around the turtle's rock,
a sea that once boiled red and black
before turning green as smoke cleared
from the skies where buzzards now soar.

Like Cézanne's Mont Sainte Victoire,
all year round Jane's painted this view
of the Auze's work on the land,
before it joins with the Lignon
and together they meet the Loire.

Painting finished, my view was sought
and I proposed the bird of prey
"to make the image more 3-D",
but now I'm not so sure, for depth
and distance were already caught.

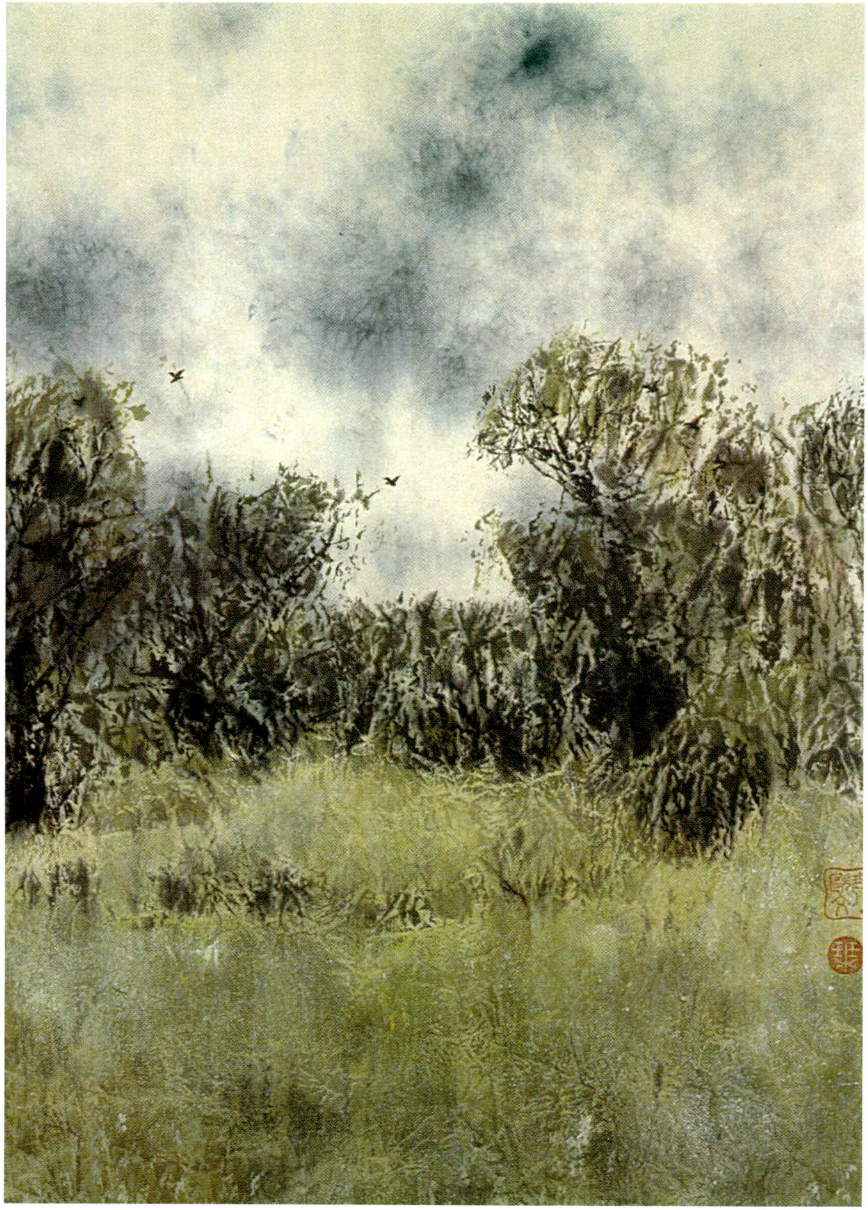

Wandlebury

Cut long before the Romans came
was Wandlebury Ring,
safe haven for Iceni clans,
a place to seat a king.

The highest point for miles around,
this hill of Gog Magog,
was circumscribed by deep ditches
and walls of splintered log.

Today a park where people come
to walk their dogs or stroll,
bring family to play fun games
up on the chalky knoll.

But trace out the Celtic circle
then turn off through the trees
and look for a sunlit meadow
touched by the softest breeze.

Lie in the grass by waiting woods
near the tangled briars;
in the earth you might smell the ash
of long dead cooking fires.

There's a whirr of wings above you;
lie still and close your eyes
and on the summer air might come
far shouts and battle cries.

Notes and Translations

RANNOCH MOOR
The quotation in the last line is from Neil Munro, *The New Road*, published in 1914.

VIEW FROM RAFFY
Suc is the local name for the dome-shaped hills of a particular geomorphological type found in large numbers in the Haute-Loire and Ardèche departments of France, but nowhere else in Europe. *Sucs*, which are of volcanic origin, consist mostly of trachyte and phonolite, the latter once widely used for roofing because it cleaves like slate. Phonolite is so named because if struck with a hard object such as a hammer, it makes a melodic ringing sound.

MEYGAL is a small massif in Haute-Loire, its highest point being the summit of Le Testavoyre at just over 4,700 ft. Raffy is a hamlet at nearly 4,200 ft and about a mile away from the summit of Le Testavoyre.

LOCH DUICH
The Chinese word *chi* means the inner spirit or essential essence and is often used in the context of Chinese painting.

OUR NEIGHBOURS' HOUSE
Some names have been changed.

NEAR POKHARA
Gompa is a Tibetan word for a meditation room, frequently used by Westerners to refer to a Buddhist monastery or holy place. *Thangka* is a Tibetan Buddhist scroll painting on cloth.

PONOT is an inhabitant of Le Puy-en-Velay.

TRINITY COLLEGE BRIDGE
Xu Zhimo was born in China in 1897. After three years of study at American universities, he spent a year at King's College, Cambridge. He adored the work of the English Romantic poets and also fell in love with Cambridge and its river. Back in his home country he became a prime mover in modern poetry and his *Taking Leave of Cambridge Again* (1928) is famous in China. One translation of the second stanza is "The golden willows by the riverside / Are young brides in the setting sun; / Their glittering reflections on the shimmering river / Keep undulating in my heart." Xu Zhimo married twice and at one time was deeply in love with a third woman, but his feelings for her were unrequited. He died in a plane crash in 1931. A stone, with an inscription in Chinese taken from his poetry, is set beside King's College Bridge.

ELY CATHEDRAL
Æthelthryth (c. 636–679 AD) was a daughter of King Anna of East Anglia. An Anglo-Saxon saint, she is also known as Etheldreda or Audrey. First married in her teens, she persuaded her husband – who had gifted her the Isle of Ely – to respect her pre-nuptial vow of perpetual virginity. After his death, Æthelthryth married Ecgfrith of Northumbria, only a boy at the time, but managed to persuade him and the bishop of York, her spiritual counselor, that she should live in a nunnery. She later had to flee from the King back to the Isle of Ely accompanied by two nuns, evading capture with the help of a rising tide (according to legend). She later became Abbess of Ely.

MOUNTAINS OF THE MIND
'Mountains of the mind' is a reference to the poem by Gerald Manley Hopkins (1844–89) titled 'No worst, there is none. Pitched past pitch of grief.' The second stanza opens with "O the mind, mind has mountains; cliffs of fall / Frightful, sheer, no man-fathomed…" The association between black dogs and dark thoughts has a long history, but is probably best known because of Winston Churchill who famously used 'black dog' as a metaphor for his depression.

The Painter and the Poet

Jane Evans

Jane studied Chinese brush painting at the Chinese Artists' Guild and the Philippine Chinese Art Center in Manila, under the tuition of Chen Bing Sun, Hau Chiok and Sy Chiu Hua. After returning to Britain, Jane continued to develop her painting, exploring the versatility of Chinese techniques and materials by using them in adventurous ways. Drawing on Eastern and Western ideas about light, space and perspective, she has evolved a highly original style, which combines both aesthetic traditions.

Jane, who is Honorary Co-president of the Chinese Brush Painters Society, has held several successful one-woman exhibitions and is in demand for commissions. She has taught many courses and held workshops in Britain and abroad. Her work has won a prize from Art Direction Magazine in the USA and also the Rosentiel Prize. She presented, by invitation, a paper on Chinese painting at a symposium at Princeton University during its 250th anniversary celebrations. She has illustrated several books, including over 80 illustrations for *The New I-Ching* by Lillian Too. Jane has been an art reviewer both in print and for BBC Radio Cambridgeshire. She and her work have also been featured on television.

Jane's first book, *Chinese Brush Painting*, Collins and Watson-Guptill, 1987, was republished in paperback by Harper Collins in 1989 and reprinted in 1991 and 1992. With American, Dutch and French editions as well, this book was the first substantial introduction for Western artists by a Western artist to the approaches and techniques of Chinese brush painting and remained the market leader for many years. Jane's other books include: *Chinese Flower Painting*, Search Press, 1990; *Landscape Painting With A Chinese Brush*, HarperCollins, 1992; and *Learn To Paint With A Chinese Brush*, HarperCollins, 1994. A new edition of her first book was published by Dover Publications Inc. in 2004.

Martin Evans

Martin's poetry publications comprise work published in 1968 in *Truth to Tell* (ed. Nancy Martin), Oxford University Press, and in *Universities' Poetry Eight* (ed. Howard Sergeant) and the story told in verse in *Song of France – Ode to the Haute-Loire*, Stamford Press, 2019.